ROAD SENSE:
The Art
of
Advanced Driving

Doug Holland

To my father, John Holland who, as well as being an outstanding driver in his own right, speaks on the subject with an enthusiasm which is at once both infectious and inspiring.

Copyright ©, D. Holland, 1993

Published by Sigma Leisure – an imprint of
Sigma Press, 1 South Oak Lane, Wilmslow, Cheshire SK9 6AR, England.

Whilst every effort has been made to ensure that the information given in this book is correct, neither the publisher nor the author accept any responsibility for any inaccuracy nor for any damage or injury howsoever caused.

British Library Cataloguing in Publication Data
A CIP record for this book is available from the British Library.

ISBN: 1-85058-333-1

Typesetting and Design by: Sigma Press, Wilmslow, Cheshire.

Diagrams and cover design: Anchor Design, Handforth, Cheshire

Printed and Bound by
Manchester Free Press Unit E3, Longford Trading Estate, Thomas Street, Stretford, Manchester M32 0JT

PREFACE

Driving is one of those subjects upon which almost everybody has something to say. The reason for this is probably that at some point in their daily lives nearly everybody comes into contact with either a driver or his driving. Pedestrians, cyclists and motor-cyclists all share our roads with the drivers of motor vehicles, and thus they, just as much as other drivers or their passengers, experience the consequences of a person's poor driving technique or their momentary lapse in concentration. They also, of course, share in the benefits of good driving technique, but, as will be explained in due course, examples of good driving tend to be less obvious and thus less widely appreciated.

To criticize a person's driving can be one of the quickest ways to lose friends. In the hope of avoiding this consequence I have attempted in this book to make only constructive criticisms of the techniques sometimes employed by drivers as they go about the task of moving around a metal box on wheels. I have endeavoured to explain not only what is the safest, and therefore correct thing to do in a given situation, but also why it is the safest thing to do.

I do not intend this book to offer advice on every conceivable driving situation. Not only is it impossible to write such a book, even if it were possible it would probably be undesirable. What I do intend the book to do is to lay down the correct principles behind each of the individual tasks which, when joined together, form this thing we know as the driving task. It is not a book for rally drivers, or racing drivers, or for anybody who believes that accidents always happen to the other person. It is a book for everybody, at whatever stage in their driving lives they happen to be, who recognizes that in the wrong hands a motor vehicle on a public road is a lethal weapon, with the capacity to wreck lives. Handled correctly, of course, it ceases to be this and becomes instead a great liberator which allows us to not only move around, over distances long or short, more or less at will, but also to derive great pleasure from doing so. I believe that as in most things, so in driving – the confidence to perform a task comes from knowledge of that task, and that the confidence breeds the pleasure.

The book is aimed primarily at drivers of motor cars. Much of its content is relevant to the drivers and operators of other forms of motorized transport used on public roads, but the only technical questions addressed refer to the design and operation of the motor car.

It may be noted that there are few direct references within the text either to current road traffic law or to the contents of the Highway Code. I never intended my book to replace other publications relating to driving, but rather to be read in conjunction with them. It is the responsibility of all drivers to be familiar with the contents of the current Highway Code and of the legislation relating to the use of their vehicle on a public road. I intend my book to build on, rather than replace, this basic information.

Finally, in the hope of preempting accusations of chauvinism I should explain that in the interests of brevity I have throughout the text referred to the driver in the male gender. There is no suggestion, either explicit or implied, that the female driver is any less capable or important than the male of the species. Rather, this was done simply in order to save me, the writer, and you, the reader, the trouble of dealing with constant references to he/she, his/her etc.

I wish you safe and pleasurable driving.

Douglas Holland

CONTENTS

1

Mirrors, Signals, Manoeuvre

or

"Back to basics"

The mirrors-signals-manoeuvre (MSM) routine is generally the first driving-oriented phrase and routine learnt by the novice driver at the beginning of a course of lessons in how to drive. It is impressed upon the novice at an early stage in the course by the instructor that this routine is the very foundation of good and safe driving. The novice is told to memorize the routine and apply it to everything that he does with a motor vehicle. As he studies The Highway Code and other motoring books, he sees it repeated numerous times, together with other statements testifying to its significance and importance. Eventually, the stage is reached where the simple phrase 'MSM' comes, for the novice, to embody everything which is correct in the art of driving.

Unfortunately, few novice drivers are taught what the phrase actually means, and even fewer are taught to drive according to it. It is those drivers who were so taught, or have been taught since, who are on the way to being called 'advanced'.

As will be seen from this and succeeding chapters, advanced driving has as its foundations this MSM routine. That is, the correct and full MSM routine, because the phrase 'mirrors-signals-manoeuvre' is actually a disarmingly simple phrase to cover what is, in fact, quite a complex problem solving procedure. It is a procedure crucial to a driver's safety, and it is one requiring a degree of skill to be fully and correctly followed. This is the reason why we call the drivers who are able to do so 'advanced'.

Mirrors

The word 'mirrors' is a shorthand expression for 'Take effective all round observation'. Before giving a signal from his vehicle or commencing a manoeuvre a driver should check on the position and movements of other road users all around his vehicle. It clearly does not make sense for him only to be required to check behind his vehicle before deciding the answer to such questions as, *"Do I need a signal?"*, *"Which signal should I give?"*, *"When is the best time to give it?"*. It is just as likely that the road users whose position and movements will govern the answer to those questions are situated in front of, to the side of, or even above or below the driver.

Thus, the observation taken by a driver prior to giving a signal or commencing a manoeuvre should be all around his vehicle. It should also be 'effective' observation because there is no point in looking and not seeing, or in looking from a place from which nothing can be seen. The object of that first step in the 'mirrors-signals-manoeuvre' routine is for the driver to look and familiarize himself with the situation all around his vehicle.

Signals

It will be seen in a later chapter that there are seven types of signal which a driver can give from his vehicle. The meanings of those signals will be discussed in that chapter, together with some thoughts on their timing and duration.

Given that the purpose of a signal is to communicate information to another road user, it follows that the term 'signal' is a shorthand expression for 'Signal if doing so would help or warn any other road user', or 'Signal if necessary'. If it is not necessary for a driver to inform or warn any other road user of his movements, proposed movements, or presence (either because that other road user already knows these things, or because they do not need to know, or because there is no other road user present), then why give a signal? If it is proposed to make a left turn, for instance, and effective all round observation reveals that there are no other road users anywhere around, a signal would clearly not be necessary and need not, therefore, be given.

An argument often levelled against this principle of 'discretionary' or 'thoughtful' signalling, and which is often said to support the principle of 'habitual' signalling (i.e. signalling for every manoeuvre irrespective of whether there is another road user to benefit from it) runs as follows: there is no harm in giving a signal which is not, strictly speaking, necessary. If it is proposed to turn left and there is nobody about, what possible danger could be caused by giving a signal?

This is a superficially appealing argument, and it is valid as far as it goes. However, it fails to take account of one important factor – human nature. It is generally found that the driver who gives a signal when a signal is not necessary is the driver who has not taken effective observation all around his vehicle and seen that a signal is not necessary. In other words, the mirrors-signals-manoeuvre routine has been abbreviated to 'signals-manoeuvre'. As will be seen later this is undesirable and potentially dangerous. On the other hand, the driver who wishes to answer the question *"Is a signal necessary?"* is the driver who is required to take effective all round observation in order to do so.

Put yet another way, if unnecessary signals are given, it is not the signal itself which is the problem (unless it is misleading); rather it is the mental attitude of the driver immediately before the application of that signal. If a signal is given which was not required, it is much more likely that the thought process of the driver immediately before its application was: *"I will not bother to take effective all round observation because I will signal no matter what I see"* rather than: *"I have taken effective all round observation, and I have satisfied myself that I know the position and movements of all other road users around my vehicle. Clearly a signal is not necessary, but I will give one anyway"*.

Another argument apparently in favour of habitual signalling is that although a signal may not be required at the commencement of the manoeuvre, before the manoeuvre has been completed, the situation may have changed and a signal become necessary.

If that were the case, then as soon as the signal became necessary the advanced driver would give it. The advanced driver realizes that if another road user happens upon the scene in the midst of the manoeuvre then that other road user would much rather see a fresh signal applied for his benefit than see a signal already operating which, as far as he knows, may have been misapplied, or applied for an earlier manoeuvre and not cancelled. Further, in order to know whether a signal has become necessary at a later stage the advanced driver must continue to take effective observation all around his vehicle. It is a temptation very infrequently resisted for the habitual signaller to cease looking once the signal has been applied.

Manoeuvre

Essentially, a manoeuvre is any change in state of the vehicle. It is a change in position of the vehicle to either the left or the right, or a variation in speed by either slowing down or speeding up.

It can thus be seen that what many drivers would consider to be a single manoeuvre, such as a left or right turn, or a stop on the left, could, in fact, be a more complicated amalgamation of two or more individual manoeuvres. In order to complete a left turn into a side road the driver may have to adjust the position of his vehicle over to the left and reduce its speed before actually turning left. For a similar right turn he may have to alter the position of his vehicle more towards the centre of the road and reduce its speed (possibly to a stop) before turning right. To make a stop on the left he may need to move his vehicle back into the near-side of the road before braking to a stop.

So, a complete definition of the phrase which forms the bedrock of the whole technique of correct, and therefore advanced, driving, and for which the expression 'mirrors-signals-manoeuvre' is merely shorthand, reads as follows: *'Take effective all round observation and consider the need for signals to help or warn other road users before altering the position or speed of the vehicle'*.

This phrase is not quite as simple as the one with which the chapter began, but it is still fairly basic. The skill of the advanced driver is revealed in his full understanding and implementation of the individual terms of that phrase.

2

Mirrors

or

"Look out, he's behind you!"

Good driving and good mirror work go hand in hand. A driver cannot attain the former without applying the latter. Therefore, *advanced* driving and good mirror work go hand in hand.

If a driver demonstrates good mirror work (that is, correct use of the correct mirrors at the correct time) he reveals an awful lot about himself. He reveals that he not only understands the basic principles of moving a vehicle around safely on a road, but also that he recognizes the responsibilities he has to other road users – responsibilities which emanate from the fact that he is but one part of a much larger scheme of things. In his vehicle on a road, he is a small fish in a big sea.

Good mirror work goes right to the heart of advanced driving. It is the roots that both support and nourish the rest of the tree.

The checks of the mirror which a driver should be making can be divided into two categories. First, there are the 'routine' mirror checks. These checks are carried out by a driver in order to catch up on the latest developments in the situation on the road behind, and they are made while he himself is continuing to simply drive along a steady course at a steady speed. These *'routine'* mirror checks should be carried out between every 5 to 10 seconds.

Second, there are those checks which must be made prior to carrying out certain actions with a vehicle. These are *'required'* mirror checks.

Before discussing *'routine'* and *'required'* mirror checks in detail, there are two general points to be made.

Firstly, it is clearly pointless a driver looking into his mirrors unless he actually sees what they are showing him. A movement of the eyes in the direction of the piece of glass called the mirror is not enough – the driver must focus on, be interested in, and take cognisance of, the picture on that piece of glass.

Secondly, having looked at the picture the driver must then ensure that he acts upon what he sees. There is no purpose whatsoever in the driver, for instance, checking the mirror before moving out to pass a stationary obstruction, noticing that there is a vehicle moving up alongside to carry out an overtake, and then pulling out anyway. In this case, acting on what he saw would have meant the driver letting the overtaking vehicle pass before moving out.

Routine Mirror Checks

It is vitally important that as a vehicle is driven along the road, the driver has continuously updated information about what is happening behind him. The reason for this is very simple – what is happening behind him could very well involve him.

If there is a vehicle moving up in preparation for an overtake, then that involves him. If the driver behind continually drives closer than is safe, then that involves him. If the previously empty road behind has now been filled by a motor cyclist, then that involves him.

In the same way as a radar would, a driver needs to be continually tracking the positions and movements of the vehicles behind. If the driver were to check his mirror and see a red van behind, but the next time he checked he had a lorry following, then at some point he has missed at least one mirror check. He does not know what happened to the red van, and he may have needed to know.

By having this regularly updated information on the situation behind, the driver can, if necessary, make much quicker decisions than he otherwise could about what it is or is not safe to do should an emergency arise. If the driver has not checked behind him for some considerable time and an emergency situation does occur, then he has two choices. Either he brakes or swerves regardless and trusts to luck, or he takes up valuable time acquainting himself with the situation behind before deciding on what action he may safely take. If that emergency had arisen shortly or immediately after a mirror check, however, then either a brief glance to confirm the situation, or indeed no glance at all, would suffice.

It would be reassuring for a driver if, whenever he had following traffic, it was people that he knew well. If that was the case he would have a good idea about what he might expect them to do in given circumstances. The likely actions of close friends and relations may often be predicted quite accurately. With good mirror work a driver may indeed get to know the drivers behind very well, even if he has never met them. By having a good look at them he may deduce a number of things. Is the following driver alert, or is his attention wandering from the driving task? Is he concentrating on what is happening in and around his vehicle, or is he perhaps busier talking to his passengers? Is he craning his neck to see around the vehicles ahead, possibly sizing up an overtake? Does he keep a consistent distance behind, or is his following distance erratic; very close one minute, way back the next? If so, can the reason be found for this?

If circumstances allow, the same questions may be asked of the drivers two and three vehicles back. The more information a driver has about his following traffic the more likely it is that he will be able to predict their behaviour. The more accurately he can predict their behaviour the less likely it is that they will involve him in any danger. With good routine mirror work, it is not unusual for a driver to have the feeling that he knew the driver behind was about to overtake even before the other driver knew.

Routine mirror checks between every 5 to 10 seconds will seem unusually frequent to a driver not used to making such full use of his mirrors. However, the benefits of such frequent and effective rear observation, both in terms of safety as nothing which happens behind takes the driver by surprise, and in terms of the peace of mind it brings, will soon be appreciated. Good routine mirror work shows that a driver understands that things behind can change very quickly, and that he appreciates that those changes could affect his safety.

Required Mirror Checks

There are a number of operations which may be carried out either in or with a vehicle that require effective rear observation before being commenced. To begin any of these operations without first having checked behind is potentially very dangerous. There are three of these such operations.

1. Signalling

As was discussed previously, virtually the first driving routine which the novice driver learns is the mirrors-signal-manoeuvre routine. It is impressed upon the novice at an early stage in the instruction that it is essential that before a signal is given from a vehicle the mirrors are checked and effective rear observation is taken.

The reason for this pre-signal mirror check is that the following question needs answering before a signal is given: Is this a suitable and safe time at which to give a signal? If the driver intends to take the next road on the right he must take effective rear observation to find out whether there is, for instance, a vehicle moving up alongside to carry out an overtake. If there is, giving a signal at that moment will probably cause the overtaking vehicle to either brake firmly and abort the overtake, or swerve, in the belief that the other driver is about to start moving to his right. The answer to the above question in these circumstances would be "No",and the driver should delay giving the signal until the overtaking vehicle has passed.

If a driver intends to take the next road on the left, before signalling by indicator the mirrors should again be checked and the above question

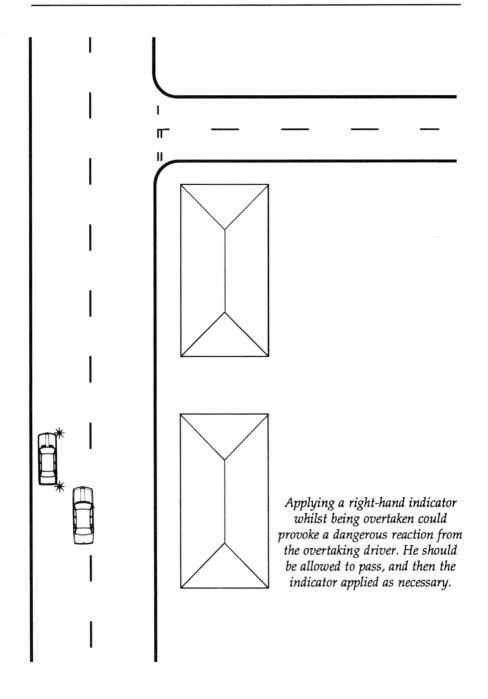

Applying a right-hand indicator whilst being overtaken could provoke a dangerous reaction from the overtaking driver. He should be allowed to pass, and then the indicator applied as necessary.

answered. As will be discussed shortly there is an implication within an indicator of an intention to slow down, and when he checks his mirrors, the driver may assess that if the following driver were to respond instantly to that implication by also slowing down, he may cause an incident behind him. In an extreme case, the driver wishing to make the turn may in fact decide to abort it for this reason. In a less extreme case, he may decide that he simply needs to create more space between himself and the following vehicle before applying the signal. Whatever the outcome of the mirror check, that mirror check needs to be made.

This principle of taking effective rear observation before giving a signal applies not only to indicators given prior to turning left or right; rather it applies to all signals given.

Before sending out messages about a proposed or current manoeuvre, the driver must check behind and to the sides to ensure that the appearance of that message will not set off an unwelcome chain of events. This check behind is of equal importance to the check in front of his vehicle to make sure that there are no circumstances ahead which require special attention. Examples of such circumstances would be where the driver intends to turn left into the next road, but delays giving the indicator until he has passed the car park entrance shortly before it, in order to reduce the chances of misleading other road users as to his real intention. Again, where the intention is to turn right the driver may decide to delay giving the signal until he has passed the parked vehicle on the left in order that the indicator is not understood simply as being a warning of an intention to pass the stationary vehicle.

2. Changing direction or position

This category of mirror check is probably the most obvious and the least controversial. It is clearly not safe to move out to pass a stationary obstruction without first checking the mirrors – there may be another vehicle overtaking at that moment.

Likewise, it is not safe to move back into the left having carried out an overtake without first taking effective rear observation; the overtaken vehicle may, for whatever reason, have chosen that particular moment to speed up and be moving alongside.

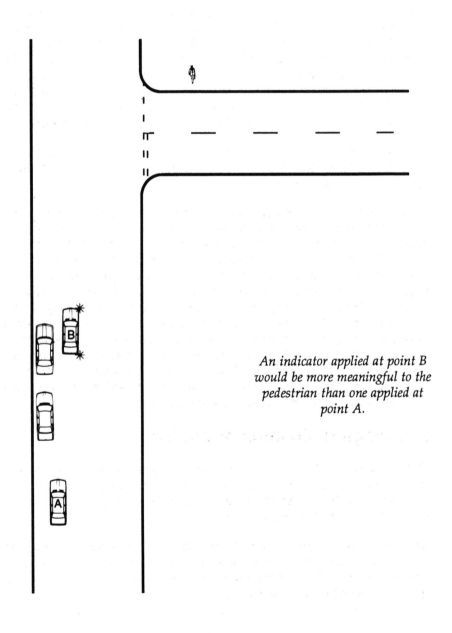

An indicator applied at point B would be more meaningful to the pedestrian than one applied at point A.

Again, it cannot be safe to move towards the centre of the road in order to avoid a pot-hole, or turn right into a driveway, or manoeuvre around some road works, without first checking behind. Any change in direction or position must be preceded by a check of the mirrors to ensure that the driver is not moving into the path of another vehicle.

3. Changing speed

Before changing the speed of his vehicle, either by slowing down or speeding up, a driver needs to check behind that it is safe to do so.

(a) Speeding up

It is poor driving practice to speed up while being overtaken. A driver should, in fact, be prepared to slow down if necessary.

This is to allow the overtaking vehicle to complete its manoeuvre as efficiently as possible. If a driver were to increase his speed as he was being overtaken he would simply lengthen the time that the manoeuvre took. This is in nobody's interests. The longer the overtaking vehicle is alongside, particularly if the overtake requires it to go onto the right-band side of the road, the more danger both drivers are exposed to.

Thus, in order to find out whether, at the time that he wishes to increase his speed, this situation applies and he is being overtaken, a driver should check his mirrors.

(b) Slowing down

Before slowing his vehicle down a driver should check behind him. The reason for this is that his decision as to when to begin slowing down, and by how much, will depend on the result of that mirror check.

Consider the hypothetical situation of a driver driving along a two lane, undivided road at the national speed limit of 60 mph. Looking ahead he sees in the distance a set of traffic lights changing to red, and he assesses the situation as being one which will require him certainly to slow down, and probably come to a stop.

Before taking his foot off the accelerator pedal (an action which in itself will begin the process of slowing the vehicle down due to engine compression) the driver consults his mirror. He sees that there is a vehicle which he also assesses, is travelling at 60 mph, very close behind. It seems to the driver that if he were to slow his vehicle down suddenly, or even just substantially within a short distance, the following driver would have very little time to react and may run into the back of him. The driver now has a problem; there is a set of traffic lights ahead showing red and he is required to stop at them.

The answer to the driver's problem is to reduce speed for the traffic lights much earlier than he would do if he did not have any close following traffic. By braking earlier, he will be able to brake more gently and lose speed more gradually. This means that his brake lights will be illuminated at a greater distance from the lights, and will give the following driver the maximum time in which to see them, assess what they mean, and respond to them by slowing his vehicle down also.

All this could be done while the first driver's vehicle is still travelling at more or less its original speed. By braking early the first driver has minimized the chances of enduring a rear end shunt.

Alternatively, having carried out a mirror check and assessed the situation as described above, the first driver may consider that his best course of action is to warn the following driver of his intention to slow his vehicle down. The only signal available to a driver which does this directly is the slowing down arm signal. If the following driver accepts the warning of the intention to slow down and begins to drop back the first driver may then brake in a conventional manner for the traffic lights.

Thus, it is essential to take effective rear observation before slowing a vehicle down. This is done in order to discover whether the situation behind requires earlier and more gentle braking than usual, or whether there are no problems and normal braking may be carried out immediately. Clearly, in order to make, this decision, and then carry out the appropriate action if necessary, a driver needs to be identifying at a very early stage the need to apply the brakes and then carrying out the mirror check.

The only exception to the rule that effective rear observation should be taken before slowing a vehicle down is in a genuine emergency situation where the priority is simply to get the vehicle stopped. For instance, if a child were to run into the road immediately in front of a vehicle. As was said above, if the driver's routine mirror work has been good up to that point he should have a good idea of the situation behind anyway, but if not he cannot afford the wasted time of a mirror check before pressing the brake pedal.

(c) The braking mirror check

It is not sufficient for a driver to check his mirrors prior to slowing his vehicle down, and then imagine that the need for rear observation is at an end. Effective rear observation should also be considered whilst the vehicle is in the process of being slowed down. In the hypothetical situation described above where the driver was approaching a set of traffic lights showing red, with close following traffic, that driver's problems would be compounded if the following driver did not respond to either the arm signal warning of a future intention to slow down, or the appearance of the brake lights meaning that the vehicle ahead was actually slowing down. If the first driver saw that, for whatever reason, the following driver was not slowing his vehicle down accordingly, he must now take measures to deal with this new problem.

Precisely what the first driver would do in the above situation depends on the exact circumstances prevailing at the time. If he had a sufficiently good view into all the other roads converging at the junction he may decide that the least dangerous course of action would be to go through the red light. This decision would not be taken lightly, but the consequences of doing so may be preferable to those resulting from a rear end shunt.

Alternatively, if there were vacant ground to either the left or the right of his vehicle the driver may decide that the best thing to do is to drive onto it in order to get out of the way.

Whatever the driver eventually decides to do, the important point is that by observing the road behind AS he reduced the speed of his vehicle, and observing the actions of the following drivers, at least he has had a chance to do something. Had he simply applied his brakes and then left the matter there he would not have been aware of the potentially dangerous situation developing behind, and his destiny would have been out of his own hands.

Which Mirror to Check?

There are no rigid rules about which mirror or mirrors should be checked. A driver should check whichever mirror or combination of mirrors will provide him with the information he requires.

The centrally located interior mirror on a car is the most frequently used, due to the fact it shows the area directly behind the vehicle. This is the area which most often needs checking. Door mirrors, when correctly adjusted, show the area along the side of the vehicle and away from it either to the near-side or the off-side.

These door mirrors, or on older vehicles the wing mirrors, though not consulted as frequently as the interior mirror, do come into their own in

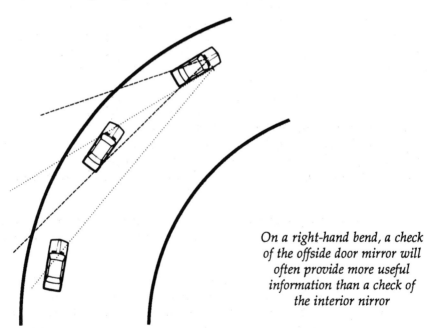

On a right-hand bend, a check of the offside door mirror will often provide more useful information than a check of the interior nirror

certain situations. For instance, the offside door mirror is probably the most useful one to check when negotiating a right-hand bend. This is due to the fact that the interior mirror would mainly just give a view of the wall or hedge along the left-hand side of the road, whereas the door mirror would reveal the view back across the bend to the road behind. Likewise, the near-side door mirror comes into its own during a left-hand bend for similar reasons.

Again, checking the off-side door mirror would be beneficial when moving away from directly in front of a large vehicle when the interior mirror would simply show a view of the front grill of the vehicle behind.

Another use of the near-side door mirror would be at a junction where the intention is to turn left and there is the possibility of a cyclist or motor cyclist moving up between the vehicle and the kerb.

There are no rules about which mirror to check. The only important thing is that the driver finds a way of checking the section of road which he feels needs checking. If that means the interior mirror then that is the one to use. If either of the door mirrors would do a better job, then those are the ones which should be checked. If a combination of the interior mirror and one or more of the door mirrors would do the best job, then they should be used.

Although the need should not arise often if a driver's mirror work is of a consistently high standard, it may be necessary for him to have a brief glance over one of his shoulders to check an area of road not revealed to him by any of his mirrors. Checking a blind spot in this way, providing it is done with due regard for the situation ahead and the speed at which his vehicle is travelling, is perfectly acceptable. If rear observation needs to be taken, then the driver should find a way of taking it.

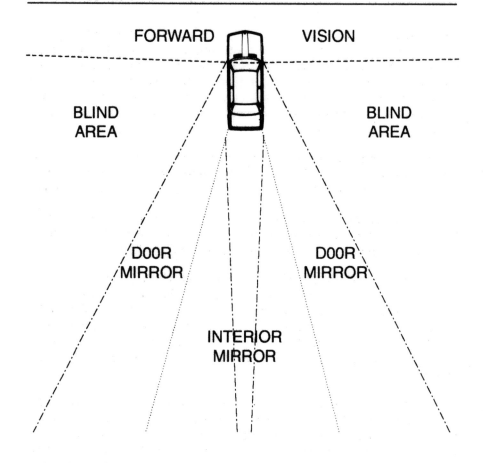

Despite having an interior mirror and two door mirrors, there is a blind spot over each of the driver's shoulders.

3

Signals

or

"Excuse me, you do know I'm here, don't you?"

The term 'signal' is an all embracing one used to describe the several and varied ways by which drivers are able to communicate with other road users. The use of signals to communicate information to other road users saves drivers the trouble of having to wind their windows down and shout over to the other person. Signals are the language of the road, and it is the responsibility of all drivers to understand them and use them correctly.

Signals which give a notice of future intention, such as a direction indicator or an arm signal, must clearly be given **before** the proposed manoeuvre is commenced. It is a pointless exercise, for instance, for a driver to give a right-hand indicator signal to warn of an intention to move to the right at precisely the same moment as he begins to move out. To make any sense, and to be in any way useful to another road user, the signal should be given before beginning to move out.

Furthermore, it needs to be understood that signals wárning of a future intention do not bring with them any absolute right to carry out that intention. Simply applying a left-hand indicator does not give a driver the automatic prerogative to turn left, move to the left, or stop on the left. The responsibility is still his to make sure it is safe to do any of these things. If it is not safe, then the fact that there is an amber coloured light flashing on the left-hand side of his vehicle does not make it safe, and the manoeuvre should not be attempted.

The question may then be posed, *"Why doesn't a signal bring with it the automatic right to carry out a manoeuvre? If a driver has warned other road users of his intended actions, why is the responsibility not now theirs to accommodate him? After all, they have been warned."*

This argument immediately collapses once it is realized that a signal not seen is a signal not given. How does a driver know that the pedestrian for whose benefit he has just indicated has seen the indicator? He does not; the pedestrian may be blind or blinded. How does he know that the cyclist for whose benefit he has just sounded his horn has heard the horn note? He does not; the cyclist may be deaf or deafened. How does he know that the driver behind, for whose benefit he has just illuminated his brake lights, has seen the lights? He does not; the driver's attention may be elsewhere, or the lights may not have illuminated.

Furthermore, even assuming that the intended recipient of the signal has seen or heard it, how does the driver know that that person has correctly understood it? A left-hand indicator has three separate and distinct meanings, a right-hand indicator two. A driver dare not assume that the other road user has put the correct interpretation on the signal.

Signals are useful and helpful only when seen and correctly understood. A driver, however, dare not assume either of these facts about any signal which he gives.

As a general rule of thumb, indicators should be allowed to flash at least three times before the proposed manoeuvre is begun. This lapse of time gives the intended recipient of the signal time in which to see it, recognize what it means, and formulate his own driving plan on the basis of it. If the time which elapses between the indicator and the commencement of the manoeuvre is less than this, then it was probably not worth indicating at all. A right-hand indicator applied by a driver as he moves his vehicle to the right is no use to the following driver – he can see that the vehicle is moving to the right.

For signals other than indicators, that is a horn note, flashed headlamps, and arm signals, then the driver should adapt the rule and allow a three second gap between the giving of the signal and the commencement of the manoeuvre. Anything less and the signal probably came too late to be of any use to anybody.

The signals available for use by a driver are as follows:

❑ Indicators

❑ Brake lights

❑ Horn note

❑ Flashed headlamps

❑ Arm signals

❑ The position on the road that he adopts

❑ The speed at which be drives.

Each of these will be examined in turn.

Indicators

Modern vehicles are fitted with very reliable, highly conspicuous indicators. It is this high degree of reliability and visibility which makes indicators, rather than arm signals, the more usual way to warn of an intention to turn or deviate.

The basic meanings which should be attached to indicators, both by the giver and the receiver of the signal, are as follows: a left-band indicator means *"I intend to turn left, or stop on the left, or move to the left"*. A right-hand indicator should be taken to mean *"I intend to turn right, or move to the right"*.

Advanced driving, however, requires that a driver has a more thorough understanding of precisely what information a particular indicator is conveying. That information will vary according to the time and the place at which the signal is given, and the person to whom it is given.

Consider the hypothetical situation of a driver driving along a conventional two lane, single carriageway road at the maximum legal speed of 30 mph. The driver intends to turn into the next side road on the left. He has one vehicle following at a safe distance, and there is one vehicle waiting to emerge and turn right from the side road. A short distance along the side road is a group of children playing a game of football in the middle of the road. At a suitable distance from his intended turn the driver checks his mirror and then gives a left-hand indicator signal. It will be seen that this indicator signal conveys different information to each of the three other groups of road users.

The following driver

The following driver is not too concerned at the moment whether the driver ahead intends turning to the left or stopping on the left. For the driver ahead to be warning of an intention simply to move to the left on a conventional two lane road, he would probably consider as unlikely, but which of the other two operations he will be carrying out does not, at this stage, concern the following driver. What does concern him and interest him is the fact that in order to either turn left or stop on the left the vehicle ahead is probably going to have to slow down.

In other words, at this stage, the left-hand indicator is conveying the same information to following traffic as a slowing down arm signal would. There is an implied suggestion within that indicator that the vehicle will shortly be slowing down.

Experienced drivers, either consciously or unconsciously, recognize this suggestion, and many of them begin immediately to either brake or move out to the right as soon as a left-hand indicator appears on the vehicle ahead. Novice drivers generally do not recognize it, and many of them get very close to a vehicle which is either turning left or stopping on the left. At a later stage in the manoeuvre, whether the indicating vehicle is either turning left or simply stopping on the left may well become relevant to following traffic, as they then need to start planning the possible overtake of a stationary vehicle. In the early stages of the manoeuvre, however, it is the implication of the loss of speed which interests following traffic.

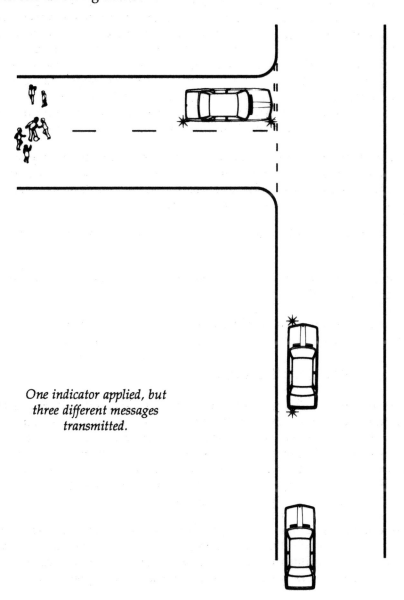

*One indicator applied, but
three different messages
transmitted.*

The emerging vehicle

The information conveyed to the driver of the emerging vehicle is a combination of the implied suggestion that the approaching vehicle will probably start slowing down shortly, and one of the more conventional meanings. That driver is interested firstly in the fact that the approaching vehicle will probably be slowing down because he may decide that this will give him enough time to safely emerge and clear the junction before the other vehicle arrives there. He is interested secondly in the fact that it will probably be either turning or stopping on the left because this fact again means that it may be safe for him to emerge.

It must be stressed here that the driver wishing to emerge at the junction may well be foolish to emerge simply on the basis of the indicator from the approaching vehicle. He does not know where the other driver intends to turn: at this road or the next one?

He does not know where he intends to stop: before the junction or after it?

Finally, he does not know for certain that the indicator has not been operated by mistake.

That said, the emerging driver has the choice of accepting or rejecting these two separate, and quite distinct, pieces of information.

The children in the road

If the children playing football in the side road see and understand the indicator, they will take from it the conventional meaning only that in all probability the approaching vehicle will shortly be turning into their road and disturbing their game. They may look on in the hope that the indicator means that the vehicle will be stopping on the left either before or after the junction, but the implied suggestion of a loss of speed on the part of the vehicle does not concern them.

Thus, one indicator signal given, but three different groups of road users taking from it three different meanings. This implied suggestion within an indicator of an intention to slow down is potentially very useful to a driver, whether he is the giver or the receiver of the signal. It is another string to his bow when either he is considering how best to communicate his intentions to his fellow road users, or attempting to interpret their signals.

Brake Lights

This signal does not generally warn of a future intention, but rather it informs other road users of something which is already happening. Brake lights are only illuminated once the brake pedal has been pressed; therefore, generally, they are only illuminated once the vehicle has begun to slow down. Even if the lights are activated before the brakes have started to bite, at the very least the driver has removed his foot from the accelerator pedal. This means that because of the effect of engine compression, the vehicle has already begun to slow down. The only exception to this would be if the driver removed his foot from the accelerator pedal very slowly whilst the vehicle was descending a steep hill. In this case the increasing pull of gravity on the vehicle may compensate for the effects of engine compression and keep the vehicle at a constant speed.

Horn note and Flashed headlamps

These signals also are not signals of future intention. They should be used to attract the attention of a road user who the driver feels is oblivious of his presence, but who he feels should not be.

The horn is the more usual method by which a driver warns of his presence, but a flash of the headlights can be used in lieu of a horn warning at night when it is either illegal or less effective to sound the horn, or at high speed, such as overtaking on the open road when the sound of a horn would either be left behind or simply not heard over the background noise.

Examples of situations where a horn note (or flash of the headlamps) might be usefully employed include: when approaching a group of children playing on the footpath; on the approach to a blind bend or brow of a hill; on the approach to a bus where there is the possibility of pedestrians stepping out from behind it.

Use of either the horn or flashed headlamps does not remove from the driver the responsibility to take every other action to ensure that a situation is dealt with safely. These two signals do not bring with them any divine right to proceed; they are simply a means of attracting somebody's attention – rather like tapping somebody gently on the shoulder and saying, *"Excuse me, you do know I'm here, don't you?"*

Whilst care must always be exercised in the use of signals because of the ever present possibility that the recipient of the signal will attribute to it a meaning different from the one intended by the giver, this is especially true if a horn note or flash of the headlamps is used.

Any deviation from the principles as contained in the Highway Code regarding the use of these signals introduces uncertainty. Therefore, in any situation where it appears that either of these signals are being given, both the giver and the receiver of the signal should ask three questions – the giver before he applies the signal, and the receiver before he acts upon it:

❏ Is there any other road user in the vicinity likely to believe that the signal is intended for him?

❏ Is the meaning of the signal clear?

❏ What would be the consequences of the signal being misunderstood, or incorrectly acted upon?

If the answers to any of the above questions suggest a danger greater than the one the driver is wishing to avert, then the signal should not be given.

As an example, consider the situation where a driver is approaching a side road off to the left. One opposing vehicle is waiting to turn right into that side road, and another is waiting to emerge and turn right out of it. If the approaching driver flashed his headlamps in an attempt to afford precedence to either driver, the potential danger of either the wrong driver reacting to the signal, or, worse still, both drivers reacting at the same time would generally outweigh any benefit which would be derived from such a signal. In a case like this, therefore, the signal should generally not be given.

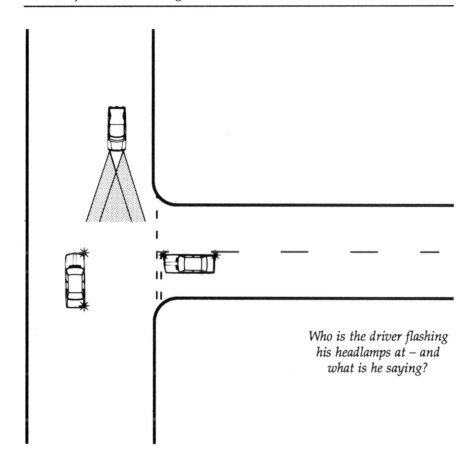

Who is the driver flashing his headlamps at – and what is he saying?

On the other hand, consider the situation where, on a road subject to a 60 mph speed limit, at three o'clock in the morning, a driver sees an opposing vehicle travelling at speed, not displaying any lights. If, having taken all round observations and establishing that there are no other road users in the vicinity, it seems that the danger of allowing the vehicle to proceed without lights outweighs any possible danger of misunderstanding etc., then in this situation often a flash may be given in an attempt to prompt the oncoming driver to display lights.

Arm Signals

Although they are not as important as they used to be, arm signals still have their place in the signals armoury of a driver. Perhaps most obviously, use would be made of them if indicators or brake lights were to fail.

They may also be used to advantage if the driver feels that he needs to confirm to another road user a signal which he has already given. For instance, if a driver intended to turn right into a side road, and prior to the turn there were one or more parked vehicles on the left, he may feel that an arm signal given after one or more of the vehicles have been passed would confirm to other road users his intention to turn rather than simply move out to pass the stationary vehicles.

The meanings, both obvious and implied as discussed previously, of the arm signals equating to our indicators are the same as for the indicators.

The slowing down arm signal is the only signal a driver has at his disposal which directly warns of an intention to slow down. As was mentioned previously, brake lights generally only inform other road users that the vehicle is slowing down.

Another advantage which this signal has over brake lights is that it may be seen from the front of the vehicle. This makes it useful in situations where it is felt advantageous to warn or inform road users ahead of the vehicle that it will be, or is, slowing, such as on the approach to a pedestrian crossing.

Position and Speed

The importance of the position which a driver adopts on the road and the speed at which he drives should not be underestimated when discussing signals sent to other drivers. A driver should understand that he is in fact signalling the whole time to other road users via these two elements.

If a driver is driving along a road at 30 mph then, because this is normally much too high a speed at which to turn left, he is signalling that he does not intend to turn into the road on the left that he is about to reach. Conversely, if he signals left prior to a side road and then proceeds to slow his vehicle down to a suitable speed at which to turn into that road, then this reduction in speed is another signal of his intention to turn and is acting to confirm the earlier left-hand indicator signal.

If a driver activates a right-hand indicator and then adopts a position towards the centre of the road, this change in position is again acting to confirm to other road users the information contained in the earlier indicator. If a driver were to activate a right turn indicator and then stay well to the left of the road, these two apparently conflicting signals may lead to confusion in the minds of other road users.

Drivers make assumptions about what other road users are more or less likely to do continually from the position they adopt on the road and the speed at which they drive. These assumptions are clearly *no more* than assumptions, and drivers should always include in their driving plans the possibility that these assumptions may be incorrect.

They should also be aware that assumptions are being made about their likely movements the whole time from the position *they* adopt and the speed at which *they* drive. Great efforts should be made to ensure that only the correct information is sent out via these two factors, and this is another convincing reason why the appropriate position and speed should be adopted well before commencing a manoeuvre. The earlier other road users receive information about a driver's intentions, the easier it will be for them to respond accordingly.

Furthermore, drivers should endeavour to send out only strong, positive messages. This is especially pertinent to the question of positioning. By adopting half-hearted positions a driver creates doubt and confusion in the minds of other road users, and often puts himself in a weak position on the road. If the road is marked in lanes then the driver should be in either one lane or the other, but he should not straddle them. He should make a decision as to the lane he requires, even if it is the wrong decision. If it proves to be the wrong decision and he is taken out of his way then he should drive around the block and find his way back onto his route.

4

Braking, Gear Changing, Accelerating and Steering

or

"May the force be with you"

To maintain control of a vehicle as it progresses along a road is to accurately balance the forces operating upon it at any given moment in time. The driver who has induced a skid in his vehicle, or otherwise lost control of it, is the driver who has failed to balance these various forces correctly.

Driving a motor vehicle is all about balance. Braking, gear changing, accelerating and steering may all apply undesirable, destabilizing forces to a vehicle, and these activities should therefore only be performed with a thorough understanding of the principles underlying them, and should at all times be carried out smoothly.

It is important to keep in mind throughout this discussion the fact that a vehicle is in its most stable condition when it is travelling along a straight and level course at a constant speed. In this state its weight is evenly distributed, and all forces acting upon it are cancelled out. In order to vary any one of these conditions, a singular or resultant force must be applied to the vehicle, a force which must be understood and controlled for that variation to be made safely.

The most stable condition is also the most desirable because, essentially, stability equals safety. If a vehicle cannot be maintained in the perfectly stable condition described above, then the aim should be to maintain it as close to it as possible, with the number and severity of any changes made to this condition kept to a minimum.

Braking

Braking and Gear Changing: the connection

It is often necessary for a driver, in the course of a journey. to reduce the speed of his vehicle. When such a situation occurs the question arises *"How best to do this?"*

The driver could simply remove his foot from the accelerator pedal. This would reduce the amount of petrol/air mixture or diesel flowing into the engine and thus reduce the amount of power that the engine produces. With the friction between the tyres and the road surface, the body of the vehicle and the air, and within the moving parts of the vehicle, remaining more or less constant, reduced engine power would result in the vehicle beginning to slow down. The vehicle would be decelerating.

However, in many circumstances, the very gentle reduction in speed afforded by deceleration is not sufficient to slow the vehicle down in time.

Therefore, the driver's foot, having been removed from the accelerator pedal, moves across and presses the brake pedal. The brake pedal is the control built into the vehicle to perform the function of slowing it down. If a vehicle needs to be slowed down more promptly than deceleration will allow, then the driver should press the brake pedal.

This point concerning the brake pedal is laboured because many drivers seem to believe that in order to slow a vehicle down it is necessary to make one or more changes down through the gear box. This is not so, and is, in fact, poor driving practice, for reasons which will be seen shortly. If a vehicle were being driven in fifth gear, for instance, and it was necessary to bring it to a stop, then, in the absence of any untoward circumstances, it should be stopped in that gear.

Once the vehicle has been slowed to the desired speed two further questions arise: firstly, *"What gear best suits this speed?"* and secondly, *"Is that gear the one presently engaged?"* If that gear is not the one engaged, the driver should at that point engage it.

The importance of having the correct gear engaged for a given speed at the moment the driver applies pressure to the accelerator pedal is generally understood. Failure to ensure this will result in the vehicle being unresponsive, uneconomical and uncomfortable.

This, then, is the only way in which the activities of braking and gear changing are connected. After having slowed down the driver may have to change down. Of course, if both the initial and new speeds were comfortably within the range of the same gear then no gear change would generally be necessary.

Principles of Braking

The brake pedal is potentially one of the most dangerous instruments in the vehicle. To use it safely a driver requires a thorough understanding of the forces which he will be applying to his vehicle when he presses it. The following principles should always be borne in mind.

❏ Brake firmly only when travelling in a straight line.

> When a vehicle is slowed, a proportion of its weight is transferred over the front wheels. The more sudden the speed loss, the larger that proportion. This is why, under heavy braking, the occupants of the vehicle lean forwards.

> This extra weight over the front of the vehicle improves the traction between the front wheels and the road surface, making

them less likely to lock and therefore skid. However, at the same time it has the detrimental effect of making the steering heavier and less responsive. With heavy, unresponsive steering both hands are required on the steering wheel. To remove one hand from the steering wheel at this point (for instance, to change gear) is courting danger.

It follows from this that under braking, there must be a reduction in the proportion of weight over the rear wheels. The rear of the vehicle in fact lifts slightly – not, under normal circumstances, enough to actually lose contact with the road surface, but it rises slightly on the suspension. The result is that the rear wheels now have reduced traction with the road surface, making them more likely to lock and therefore skid, or simply begin sliding.

Now consider what happens when a vehicle is driven along a curved path, for instance around a corner or bend. A proportion of the weight of the vehicle is transferred over the wheels on the outside of the curve, and there is a corresponding weight reduction over the wheels on the inside of the curve.

There is now only a reduced amount of adhesion between these inside wheels and the road surface, again making them more likely to skid. Thus, on a right-hand bend a proportion of the weight is shifted over the near-side wheels and all the passengers lean to the left. The tighter the curved path, the greater the weight transfer.

If the effects of braking and driving around a curved path are combined the resulting weight transfer is proportionately more destabilizing. If a driver were to brake, for instance, whilst driving around a right-hand bend, there would be a weight transfer over the front nearside wheel of the vehicle. There would, therefore, be a corresponding weight reduction over the rear off-side wheel. This wheel is now the one most likely to lose traction with the road surface if either the braking or the steering is too harsh. The reduction in the grip of this wheel is greater than it would be if either the reduction in the speed or the change of direction had been carried out individually.

At even moderate cornering speeds, the reduced weight over the inside wheel is obvious, as seen in this sequence.

Thus, the safest technique is to reduce speed whilst the vehicle is travelling in a straight line. By the time the bend or corner is reached the necessary speed reduction should have been made. In this way there is only one detrimental and destabilizing force being applied to the vehicle at any one time – first the reduction in speed, then, quite separately, the change in direction.

Many drivers brake while negotiating a bend or turn, and generally they experience no adverse consequences from so doing. This is due to the high standard of handling and road holding afforded by modern vehicles. They turn the corner safely in spite of the driver's technique, not because of it. It is in circumstances where conditions are not ideal, such as on a wet road surface, or a patch of wet leaves, or on ice, where the flaw in their technique is found out. It could, of course, also be found out in ideal conditions if either the steering movement or the reduction in speed were severe enough.

❏ Vary the brake pressure according to the quality of the road surface.

When the brake pedal is pressed the driver is relying on the friction between the wheels and the brake discs/drums which he brings into contact with them to lose the speed. The speed energy is lost in the form of heat. This frictional force, however, must never be allowed to become stronger than the frictional force present between the tyres and the road surface. When this does happen the wheels of the vehicle lock, i.e. cease revolving, and go into a skid.

Thus, the less the grip between the tyres and the road surface the less the force it would take to overcome that grip, and consequently the less brake pressure which may be safely applied.

The following will all reduce the amount of grip or traction between a road wheel and the road surface: loose chippings, water, snow, ice, wet leaves, oil deposits, mud. The amount of grip present will also depend on the quality of the tyre.

A vehicle whose wheels have locked and are skidding along the road surface is, by definition, out of control. It is also taking longer to come to a stop than one whose wheels are almost at the point of locking, but have not quite done so.

It is a fallacy believed by many drivers that the quickest way in which to stop their vehicle is to lock the wheels and skid to a stop. In fact, the vehicle reduces speed at the greatest rate when the wheels have almost, but not quite, locked. Anti-lock Braking Systems fitted to vehicles work on this principle by unlocking and then re-applying the brakes many times a second, thus maximizing the amount of time the wheels spend in the 'almost locked' state.

A driver can simulate the advantages of ABS by using the technique of cadence braking. 'Cadence' means rhythm, and this technique involves pumping the brake pedal with rhythm, releasing it immediately it is felt that the wheels have locked. If the pumping of the brake pedal were timed to coincide with the transfer of the weight of the vehicle over the front wheels as the front of the vehicle rises and then falls again, maximum traction and therefore braking effect would be enjoyed.

❑ Brake in plenty of time.

Unless a vehicle hits a very substantial object it will not come to a dead stop. Rather, time will elapse and distance will be covered as it gradually slows down. How far it will travel before coming to rest will depend essentially on two things: how fast it was travelling in the first place, and how large a braking force is applied to it.

However, in the normal course of driving there is another consideration which a driver must have in relation to how much distance he requires to stop his vehicle, and this consideration becomes relevant even before the brake pedal is touched. This is the driver's reaction time, or thinking distance.

The time that it takes a driver to react to a situation, and consequently the distance that he will have travelled before doing so, depends upon his physical and mental condition (tiredness, illness and stress may all increase it) and the amount of concentration he is applying. This 'thinking distance' will be proportional to the speed at which he is travelling. If a driver is aware that he is in any way under par and his reactions are dulled, albeit only slightly, then he should drive accordingly and leave himself more time than usual in which to slow down.

The table of stopping distances shown in The Highway Code is based upon a driver reaction time of about 0.7 second. These stopping distances should not only be learnt by heart, but the driver needs also to be able to recognize them in real situations.

Braking in Thirds

A driver's braking technique is relevant to both the safety of the drive he produces, and also to its smoothness. As has been seen, pressing the brake pedal induces a weight transfer in the vehicle. The driver's aim should always be to make that transfer smooth and progressive rather than sudden and lurching. By doing this he will minimize the risk of its overcoming the grip of the tyre on the road surface.

The initial pressure on the brake pedal should be light. This is to ensure that the retarding force brought to bear on the vehicle is applied gently, and also that the vehicle's brake lights illuminate with the vehicle travelling fairly close to its original speed.

Once the lights have been illuminated and the force introduced the pressure on the pedal may be progressively increased, the foot carrying out a 'squeezing' action.

If the driver has judged a stop correctly he should be able to gradually relax the amount of pressure on the pedal so that at the moment the vehicle comes to a halt that pressure is negligible. The stop itself, unless made on an incline, should not be felt by the occupants of the vehicle.

This braking technique, where the initial and final stages involve little pressure on the pedal and the majority of the work is done in the middle stage, is called braking in thirds.

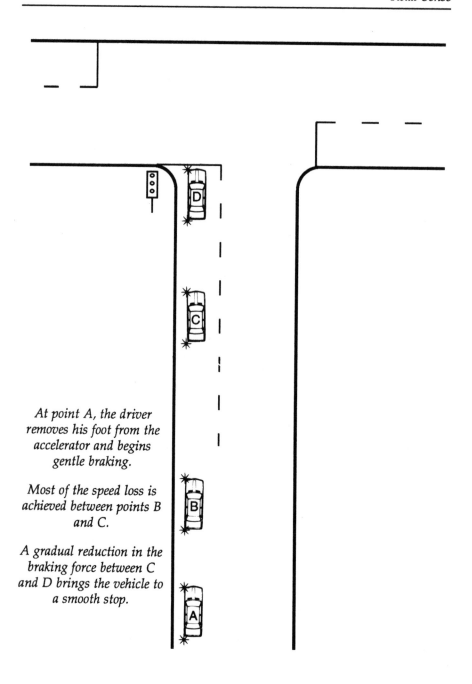

At point A, the driver removes his foot from the accelerator and begins gentle braking.

Most of the speed loss is achieved between points B and C.

A gradual reduction in the braking force between C and D brings the vehicle to a smooth stop.

Engine Braking

Generally speaking, the lower the gear engaged the greater the braking effect which will be felt from the engine when pressure is removed from the accelerator. Under braking, the torque of the pistons acts to 'soak up' some of the road speed, and this effect is more pronounced in the lower gears. Therefore it is often desirable to select a lower gear on the approach to a hazard in order to maximize the potential not only of acceleration, but also of engine braking, should braking be necessary.

The assistance of engine braking will only be effective while the clutch is engaged. Depressing the clutch pedal and disengaging the engine from the road wheels removes the effect. Thus, even in an emergency, when braking the clutch pedal should be left untouched until either it is necessary to depress it in order to avoid the engine stalling, or it is decided that no more braking is necessary and a gear change is to be made. To depress the clutch pedal earlier than necessary is to remove from the wheels the effect of engine braking earlier than necessary. This could fatally increase stopping distances.

The effect of engine braking is often very beneficial when descending a steep hill. The lower gear acts to hold the vehicle back, often avoiding the need for prolonged periods of braking and thus reducing the chances of the driver overheating his brakes and experiencing brake-fade. Brake fade occurs when the materials comprising the brakes overheat and cease to perform at their usual level of efficiency. When it occurs the vehicle can be felt to speed up, in spite of the fact that the brake pedal is being pressed. Brake fade is more likely in drum brakes than disc brakes, the latters design making them more efficient at dispersing the heat generated by braking.

It is often heard said that on poor quality road surfaces, and especially on ice, it is safer to change down through the gears in order to slow the vehicle down rather than use the brake pedal. This is only half correct.

It is true that the retarding effect of engine braking, in other words deceleration, may be more gently applied than use of the brake pedal under certain conditions, and doing so would therefore be less likely to induce a skid, but it should not be thought that actually using the gear change itself to retard the vehicle is a good technique. This is something completely different, and should be avoided for reasons which will now be discussed.

Gear Changing

In a vehicle with manual transmission the gear lever is provided in order that the driver may select the gear that best suits the speed of his vehicle at any given moment. The most suitable gear is the one which provides the most usable power without causing the engine to strain or overwork.

Whilst it is true that the effects of engine braking are greater the lower the gear, the benefits in terms of this derived from engaging successively lower gears as a vehicle's speed drops, in other words carrying out a 'ladder' change, are outweighed by the disadvantages of so doing. The main disadvantages are as follows:

❏ The driver's hands spend unnecessary time away from the steering wheel;

❏ Any retarding effect is not distributed evenly over the four wheels;

❏ Braking distances become more difficult to judge with repeated depressions of the clutch pedal;

❏ Unnecessary wear and tear is inflicted on the vehicle and driver.

Thus, the importance of matching the gear to the road speed only becomes relevant once the pressure is removed from the brake pedal and re-applied on the accelerator. At this point, if the correct gear is not engaged the vehicle will be unresponsive, uneconomical and uncomfortable.

A driver should aim to make all his gear changes smoothly and efficiently. This keeps wear and tear to a minimum, reduces petrol consumption, and ensures that the clutch pedal is depressed (and the vehicle thus coasting) for the minimum amount of time.

A positive but not over-tight grip of the gear lever should be taken, with the lever being 'palmed' in the direction of the new gear when a change is made. Smooth gear changes will be achieved by accurate rather than forceful movements of the gear lever.

When changing into a lower gear the driver may need to re-apply pressure to the accelerator pedal prior to re-engaging the clutch in order to accurately match the engine revs to the new road speed. The greater the amount by which the new road speed exceeds what might be termed the 'natural' speed for that gear, the greater the amount of pressure it will be necessary to apply.

Failure to accurately match the engine revs to the new road speed will result in a 'drag' being felt as the clutch is re-engaged (there will often be an accompanying whine from the engine). This 'drag' will further reduce the speed of the vehicle, but it is an undesirable retarding force to employ as it is generally only being applied to one axle of the vehicle – the front axle in a front wheel drive vehicle and the rear axle in one fitted with rear wheel drive.

Indeed, in circumstances where one of the driving wheels has significantly less adhesion with the road surface than the other (where one of them is on a patch of ice, for instance), the retarding force will, unless the vehicle is fitted with a limited slip differential, only be applied to the wheel on the driving axle with the reduced traction. Any force applied to a vehicle should be applied as evenly as possible over the whole vehicle in order to minimize the risk of fatally destabilizing it. Utilizing this 'drag', whether deliberately or not, to slow the vehicle down is less preferable than using the foot-brake because the foot-brake applies a retarding force over all four wheels of the vehicle.

It is undesirable to change gear while braking, because, as has been seen, a vehicle is destabilized to some degree while being slowed, and a less than perfect gear change will exacerbate this situation. With the driver's right foot on the brake pedal it cannot be on the accelerator matching the engine revs to the new road speed as explained above. A gear change made while braking is, therefore, likely to be less than perfect. There are degrees of imperfection, of course, and providing the overlapping of brake and clutch takes place at the lower end of the speed curve, then generally no undesirable consequences result.

It is clear from this discussion of good gear changing technique that many drivers make many more gear changes than are either necessary or desirable. Every gear change made involves time that one of the driver's hands spends away from the steering wheel; time that the clutch pedal spends depressed, thereby reducing the control which the driver has over his vehicle; wear and tear on the components of the gear box and the clutch; wear and tear on the driver. All these are undesirable conditions for a driver to induce, and consequently he should aim to keep the number of gear changes made to a minimum.

Ideally he should aim to make just one gear change for each hazard he encounters as he drives along the road. If he approaches a traffic light showing red in top gear then he should slow down and stop in that gear, and then, at the appropriate time, make the change into first gear to move off again. If he approaches a blind bend on a road along which he is travelling at, say, 60 mph, then he should use the brake pedal to reduce the speed of his vehicle to that appropriate for negotiating the bend, and then engage the appropriate gear for that speed. If he intends to turn into the next side road on the left he should, if necessary, use the brake pedal to reduce the speed of the vehicle to that appropriate, and then make the change into the most suitable gear for that speed. The correct driving technique is for the driver to omit intermediate gears.and to change from the gear he is in to the gear he requires for his new road speed.

Acceleration

The expression 'to accelerate' is generally used to describe an increase in road speed of a vehicle. Increasing its road speed applies precisely the opposite forces to the vehicle as does decelerating and braking to reduce its road speed.

Thus, when a vehicle is accelerated a proportion of its weight is transferred over the rear wheels. This results in good contact and adhesion between these wheels and the road surface, but reduced contact and adhesion between the front wheels and the road surface. As with braking, this less than perfectly stable condition may be undesirable as the vehicle negotiates a curved path. With the reduction in weight over the front wheels the steering becomes lighter and more responsive.

However, the term 'to accelerate' may also be used to describe an increase in pressure on the accelerator pedal without a corresponding increase in road speed from the vehicle. This could occur, for instance, where the driver finds it necessary to apply pressure to the accelerator pedal in order to maintain a constant speed as the vehicle begins to climb a hill, or as it begins to turn through a curved path, such as a corner or bend.

In this latter situation, were the driver to enter and drive around the corner or bend with the same amount of acceleration applied as he had on the straight previously when he maintained a constant speed, then he would have found that his vehicle slowed down as it negotiated the curve. Negotiating a curved path 'soaks up' some of a vehicle's road speed, and in order to maintain a constant speed the driver would need to increase the amount of acceleration applied.

The one exception to this principle of applying acceleration in order to maintain a constant speed as a vehicle negotiates a curved path would be the situation where the curved path is also downhill, and gravity may be used to provide the 'pull' necessary to avoid the vehicle being slowed.

As with the amount of brake pressure that may be safely applied to a vehicle, so the amount of acceleration which may safely be applied depends on the quality of the road surface and the amount of adhesion between it and the tyres. A driver is more likely to induce a wheel spin through clumsy use of the accelerator pedal on a road surface subject to surface water, wet leaves, loose chippings, snow, ice, etc.

Acceleration Sense

It has been seen previously that a vehicle is in its most stable condition when it is travelling at a constant speed, as this is the time when its weight is most evenly distributed. The advanced driver uses the accelerator pedal very delicately and very precisely in order to maximize the amount of time his vehicle spends in this state.

A driver should aim to develop good acceleration sense. Acceleration sense is the ability of the driver to vary the speed of his vehicle to meet changing road and traffic conditions without recourse to the brake pedal, but rather simply with use of the accelerator pedal. The advanced driver, for instance, would relax the pressure on the accelerator pedal early enough for his vehicle to decelerate to the correct speed for the next bend, whereas the non-advanced driver would keep the pressure on the accelerator longer and then have to brake.

Again, the advanced driver would not apply such firm acceleration when leaving one traffic hold-up that a stop at the next becomes inevitable. Rather, he would accelerate away more gently from the first one, with the probability then that by the time he reaches the second the problem will have been resolved and he may progress without having to bring his vehicle to a stop.

Good acceleration sense requires from the driver the ability to plan ahead. Poor acceleration sense is generally displayed by the driver who is looking only a very short distance ahead of his vehicle (in the situation above, he probably would not even have seen the second hold-up), and who is planning for only the next two or three seconds.

Steering

It is an obvious fact that in order to drive safely, and in order to be considered 'advanced', a driver must be able to control precisely the direction in which his vehicle travels and the position which it adopts on the road. A good steering technique will maximize a driver's chances of doing this, whereas a poor one will manifest itself in directions and positions being adopted which were not intended.

Furthermore, a good steering technique maximizes a driver's chances of responding satisfactorily to an emergency, and minimizes the physical effort exerted during a journey in steering the vehicle.

Good steering technique is based upon having the correct hand position on steering wheel. The correct hand position is based upon a good seating position.

The driver, on entering a vehicle, should ensure that the seat is so adjusted that all foot and hand controls are within easy reach, and not necessitating a lean forwards, but are not so close that arm movement is restricted and the body position 'bunched'. He should sit with his shoulders and bottom placed firmly against the back of the seat.

From this seating position the hands should be placed on the steering wheel in a 'ten to two' position, these figures relating to an imaginary face of a clock. If the seating position is correct this will result in the arms being slightly bent, but not hunched, at the elbow.

The fingers should be wrapped around the wheel with the thumbs placed along the inside rim. The steering wheel should be gripped positively but not over-tightly as this will induce tension and muscle fatigue in the arms and reduce control generally. The grip should, however, be tightened when cornering or braking, or when negotiating an uneven road surface.

Holding the steering wheel in this way in the 'ten to two' position offers a driver the following advantages:

❏ It allows the driver instant access to the position on the steering wheel from which maximum accurate leverage in either direction may be obtained, i.e. the position at the top of the wheel, and it means that the driver's hands are already in a position of near maximum leverage.

❏ Minor variations in the vehicle's direction, such as those caused by a cross wind or a variation in the road surface, may be rectified accurately and instantly with a slight increase in the pressure exerted by the appropriate hand.

❏ It is the best position from which to commence the *'pull, push'* method of steering.

❏ It ensures that the driver is sitting square-on to the direction of travel, and that unwanted and potentially dangerous body movement during cornering or skidding is minimized.

The *'Pull, Push'* technique

The 'pull, push' method of turning the steering wheel, whereby the steering wheel is fed through the hands in the direction of the turn, with the driver pulling down and pushing up alternately and both hands doing an equal amount of work, is the safest way in which to steer a vehicle. It offers the following advantages over other methods:

❑ It ensures that both hands remain in contact with the steering wheel during the steering operation, with the hand which is not working at a particular moment sliding around the rim to its new position;

❑ It ensures that one hand remains on each side of the wheel at all times;

❑ Accuracy in the amount of steering movement applied or removed (for this method should also be used when straightening the front wheels after the turn has been made) is maximized, as is the smoothness with which it is applied or removed;

❑ It ensures that should the driver make a turn and then, due to previously unforeseen consequences, find that he now has to apply yet more steering in the same direction, he will be able to do so. If the driver were to meet the emergency situation with his hands in the crossed position he would need to untangle them from each other and from the steering wheel before he was able to apply additional steering;

❑ As with the basic position of 'ten to two', this steering method ensures that the driver is at all times firmly seated square-on to his direction of travel;

❑ It ensures that at the apex of the turn being made the driver's hands are in the 'ten to two' position on the wheel.

The 'pull, push' steering technique is not the most efficient way in which to turn a steering wheel. It may be turned more rapidly in other ways, notably using the palm of one hand placed on the rim, or by alternately pulling down from the 12 o'clock position with each hand.

However, the 'pull, push' method does offer the best compromise between speed of turning the wheel and safety. The two alternative techniques offer very high speed turning but very little control, while pulling and pushing offers high speed turning and total control.

Cornering forces induced by steering

When the driver turns the steering wheel from the straight ahead position to either the left or the right, he is asking the vehicle to cease travelling in a straight line and to adopt the curved path dictated by the new direction of the front wheels.

However, it is the natural state for any moving object to continue in a straight line. This is clearly demonstrated when a stone is twirled around on the end of a piece of string and the string is then released – the stone flies off in a straight line (a tangent) in the direction in which it was travelling at the precise moment it was released.

In this example it is the tension present in the length of string which keeps the stone in its circular orbit as it is twirled around. There may come a point, however, where the stone is travelling at such a high speed that there is insufficient tension available in the string to hold it in that orbit, and the string snaps. The stone then flies off at the tangent.

When a vehicle is turned through a curved path it is the adhesion resulting from the friction between the tyres and the road surface which is performing the function of restraining the vehicle from continuing to travel in a straight line, and instead turn through the curve. However, in precisely the same way as at some point the string restraining the stone will snap if the stone is twirled quickly enough, so there will come a point where a vehicle is driven round a bend or turn at such a high speed that this adhesion between the tyres and the road surface is overcome and the vehicle slides forward in a straight line, completely ignoring the attempt by the front wheels to turn it.

As has been seen earlier, the amount of friction present between the tyres of a particular vehicle and the road surface will vary depending on, amongst other things, the condition of the road surface. On suspect road surfaces only reduced amounts of friction are available compared with surfaces of good quality, and a vehicle may overcome this adhesion at a correspondingly slower speed, or when making a correspondingly less severe turn. Therefore, when making turns on poor quality road surfaces lower speeds are required and steering movements must be smooth and delicate rather than snatched or clumsy.

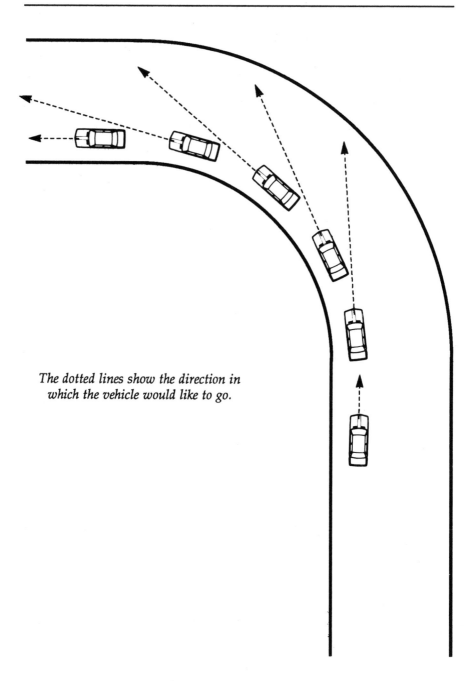

The dotted lines show the direction in which the vehicle would like to go.

The above brief explanation of the theoretical principles behind cornering is, in practice, rather simplistic. Situations where all four wheels of a vehicle lose their grip on the road surface simultaneously due solely to a driver's high speed while negotiating a turn or bend are, in practice, infrequent. More often tyres lose their grip either individually or in pairs, and the reason for the loss of grip is more involved than simply speed alone. The reason is generally basic speed plus one or more of the following:

❏ coarse acceleration

❏ coarse braking

❏ coarse steering

In terms of the demand placed on the ability of the tyres to grip the road surface, the extra destabilizing forces induced by these actions are, in effect, the straws which break the camel's back.

In other words, in the middle of the corner or bend the driver then does something else to upset the balance of the vehicle.

The emphasis on the term 'coarse' should be noted. As was stated previously, driving a vehicle is all about balance. Balance in any situation, driving or otherwise, is much more likely to be lost by coarse, snatching, movements. The advanced driver aims to get his vehicle to 'flow' around a corner or bend with deliberate, fluid movements of all the controls. In this way the chances of upsetting the delicate balance which is present when a vehicle corners at high speed are minimized.

If a driver does find himself in difficulty as he negotiates a bend due to excessive speed he is simply pouring fat on the fire if he then attempts to rectify the situation with any of (a), (b) or (c) above, for the reasons of weight distribution described earlier in the chapter. More useful would be for him to bear in mind the principle, also stated earlier, that a turning vehicle will lose speed if the power input remains constant, and he should thus consider keeping his right foot still, at a level where no further power is added. As the speed of the vehicle is lost, so some grip from the tyres becomes available for *mild* steering or braking.

An understanding of the principles involved in turning a vehicle through a corner or bend is crucial to full mastery of the art. However, this is not intended to suggest that the advanced driver negotiates any turn, let alone *most* turns, anywhere near these limits of adhesion.

The principles involved are taken to their extremes by racing drivers and rally drivers who spend much of their time approaching and then exceeding 'the limit'. The whole technique of advanced driving, however, is to avoid ever getting anywhere near the limit, so that safety margins are always kept nice and healthy.

Thus, the advanced driver will recognize in plenty of time the approach of a sharp left-hand bend and will lose excess speed well before commencing the turn, so that he may negotiate it at the ideal constant speed quite safely.

The non-advanced driver will fail to recognize it, enter it too fast and near the limit, be pushed towards the off-side of the road, and then have to hope that there is not an oncoming vehicle travelling towards the centre of the road.

The advanced driver will identify well in advance the patch of wet leaves, or oil, or ice on the road adjacent to the next side road, and bring his speed down accordingly in plenty of time. The non-advanced driver will not recognize it, but will drive over it at the same speed as he maintained previously and then have to hope that nobody emerges unexpectedly from the side road to cause him to have to brake or steer.

5

Positioning

or

"If not here, then where?"

It should be a driver's aim always to have his vehicle in the correct position on the road. The correct position on the road for a vehicle to occupy at any given moment in time is the one which gives the driver the greatest margin of safety in relation to the dangers which he has identified as existing at that time. Where two or more positions offer equal margins of safety then the one which provides maximum progress along the road is chosen.

Thus, a driver should aim to position his vehicle as far away as possible from any source of danger which he has identified, but not so far that he then exposes himself to danger from another source.

It may be seen, then, that positioning is always a matter of compromise. In determining the correct position for his vehicle to be in, the driver must make a series of trade-offs between the advantages and disadvantages of occupying a certain place on the road. In one instance, for example, a driver may decide that the advantages of moving his vehicle slightly to the left outweigh the disadvantages, and he would therefore

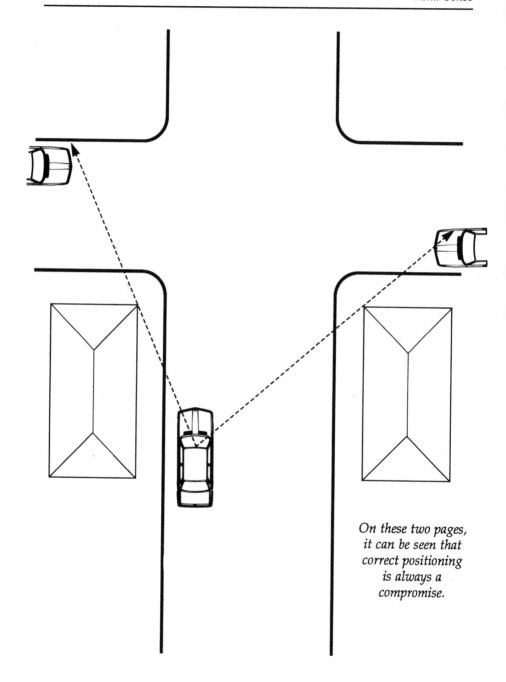

*On these two pages,
it can be seen that
correct positioning
is always a
compromise.*

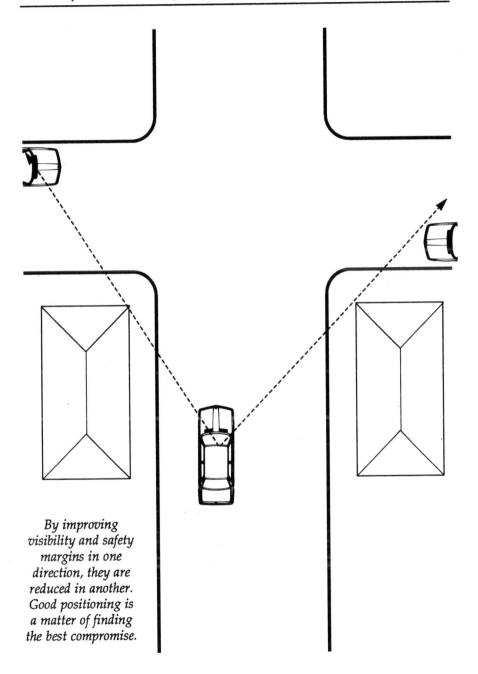

By improving visibility and safety margins in one direction, they are reduced in another. Good positioning is a matter of finding the best compromise.

make that change in position. In another situation he may decide that although in certain respects it would be advantageous to move his vehicle more to the right, in others it would not, and so on the whole the move is not worth making.

Assessing correctly the relative advantages and disadvantages of a certain position, or of a certain position change, requires skill and experience. It should be remembered, however, that a driver always has a choice about precisely whereabouts he puts his vehicle on the road, even if it is a choice between his current position and one only six inches to either the left or the right. If that position change of six inches would be advantageous, then it should be made.

Basic Principles

The following principles should be borne in mind by a driver assessing his position on the road, as they apply to all situations and all manoeuvres.

❑ The further into the left the vehicle is positioned the closer it will be to any dangers present on the near-side of the road, e.g. pedestrians, parked vehicles, side roads, driveways, but the further away it will be from any present on the off-side.

The further towards the right-hand side of the road the vehicle is positioned the closer it will be to any dangers present on the off-side of the road, e.g. oncoming vehicles, parked vehicles, side roads, driveways, but the further away it will be from any on the near-side.

❑ The further into the left the vehicle is positioned the less the opportunity for, and likelihood of, another vehicle, e.g. motor cycle, pedal cycle, overtaking along its near-side, but the greater the opportunity for, and likelihood of, another vehicle overtaking along its off-side.

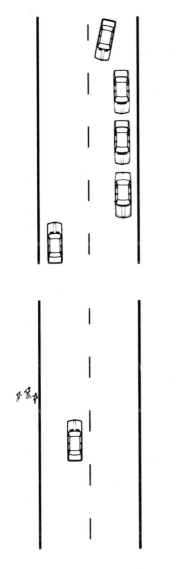

Dangers on the offside require a position to the left to be adopted. When the danger is in the nearside, a more central position would give a greater safety margin.

The further towards the right-hand side of the road the vehicle is positioned the less the opportunity for, and likelihood of, another vehicle overtaking along its off-side, but the greater the opportunity for, and likelihood of, another vehicle overtaking along its near-side.

❑ The further into the left the vehicle is positioned the more restricted will be the driver's view into many possible areas of danger along the near-side, e.g. side roads, driveways, areas behind parked vehicles, but the greater will be his view into similar areas to the off-side.

The further towards the right-hand side of the road the vehicle is positioned the more restricted will be the driver's view into many possible areas of danger along the off-side, e.g. side roads, driveways, areas behind parked vehicles, but the greater will be his view into similar areas along the near-side.

When these principles are applied to the manoeuvres of turning left and turning right, the conclusion generally reached is

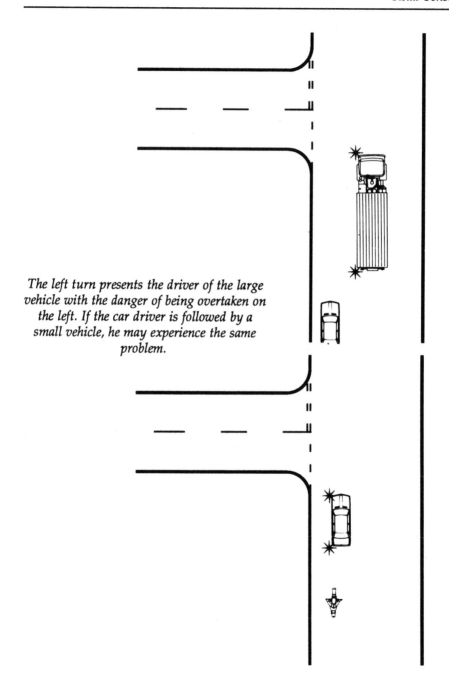

The left turn presents the driver of the large vehicle with the danger of being overtaken on the left. If the car driver is followed by a small vehicle, he may experience the same problem.

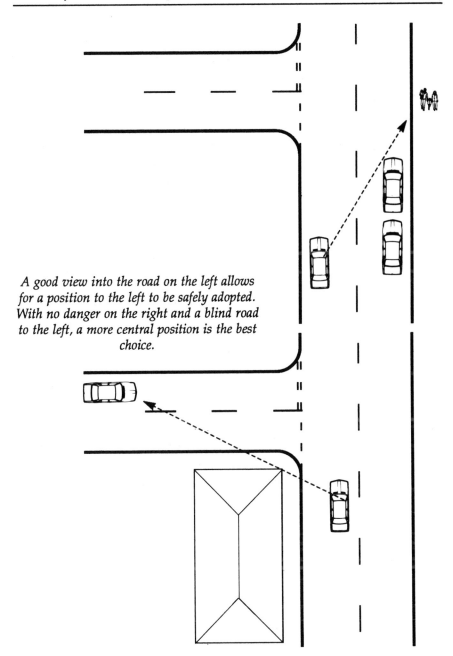

A good view into the road on the left allows for a position to the left to be safely adopted. With no danger on the right and a blind road to the left, a more central position is the best choice.

that the former is best carried out from a position towards the left edge of the road, and the latter from one up to, but not across, the centre of the road. However, situations sometimes arise where one or more of these principles assumes greater importance than normal and results in the driver adopting an unorthodox position on the road from which to carry out his intended manoeuvre.

For example, when turning right from a side road onto a main road it is the second principle above which primarily dictates that a position up to the centre of the road is adopted – by so doing the driver minimizes the chances of a following vehicle overtaking along his off-side, and maximizes the opportunity for traffic turning left to move between himself and the edge of the road and complete their turn.

When turning out of a very narrow road, however, the driver may decide that even should he adopt the conventional position up to the centre of the road then there would still not be sufficient room along the near-side of his vehicle for other traffic to progress, and that by in fact staying more to the left than usual he would at the same time both put himself further away from other traffic turning into the road (first principle above) and improve his view of traffic approaching from the right (third principle above). Here then, the driver would probably decide to carry out the turn from a position well into the left. This is illustrated on pages 60 and 61

Again, when turning left into a side road, the second principle predominates to dictate a position towards the left edge of the road – a vehicle overtaking along the near-side at this moment would be disastrous, and non-turning traffic wishes to continue by overtaking along the offside.

However, if at a particular turn the driver identifies an unusual amount of danger on the left, e.g. children playing by the kerb, or a quantity of broken glass in the road, and finds that in spite of all other measures (reducing speed even further, sounding the horn) it is not safe to pass close to these, then the first principle would now dictate that a more central position in the road than normal is adopted. Of course, great care would be taken that the risks from so doing do not materialize. If there were any suggestion that they were about to, and, for instance, a motor cyclist moved up along the near-side of the vehicle, then consideration would have to be given to abandoning the turn.

When following the road ahead at a junction then in the absence of road markings dictating the use of a particular lane there is no one principle which, more often than not, is of greater importance than the others. The driver must weigh their relative importance at that particular junction at that particular time, and then decide which is the safest place on the road for him to be.

When simply driving along the precise circumstances prevailing at the time will dictate the position to be adopted. The presence of pedestrians close to the edge of the road would suggest a position towards the centre of the road, whilst on another occasion, the approach of oncoming vehicles may require a move towards the left in order to maintain a safe gap. Again, given that in the absence of specific circumstances overtaking should be carried out on the right, the presence of other drivers who may wish to overtake him may also require of a driver a position more in to the left of the road than he would adopt in the absence of those overtaking drivers.

As a final illustration of how the correct position on the road should be assessed and adapted to suit the prevailing circumstances, on a country lane the driver may decide that in the absence of any other road user the safest place to travel is along the centre of the road, equidistant from dangers to the right and left. If one side of the road later threatened more danger than the other, then the appropriate change in position may be made.

It is vital for the driver always to be aware that, as discussed in Chapter 3, 'Signals', the position he selects for his vehicle on the road is in itself a form of communication with other road users. If he ever finds that the best position from which to perform a manoeuvre is one other than the conventional position for that manoeuvre, then care must be taken that other road users do not respond to the position actually adopted in a way which causes danger.

For instance, in the example given of the left turn into the side road where there is an inordinate amount of danger present on the left side of the road and the driver decides to complete the manoeuvre from a more

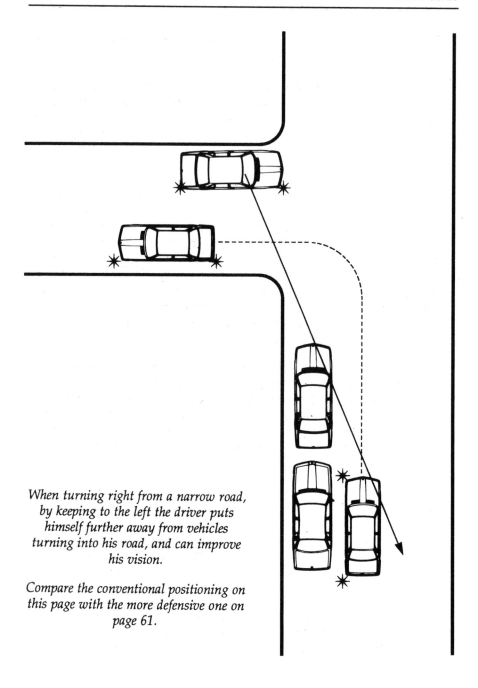

When turning right from a narrow road,
by keeping to the left the driver puts
himself further away from vehicles
turning into his road, and can improve
his vision.

Compare the conventional positioning on
this page with the more defensive one on
page 61.

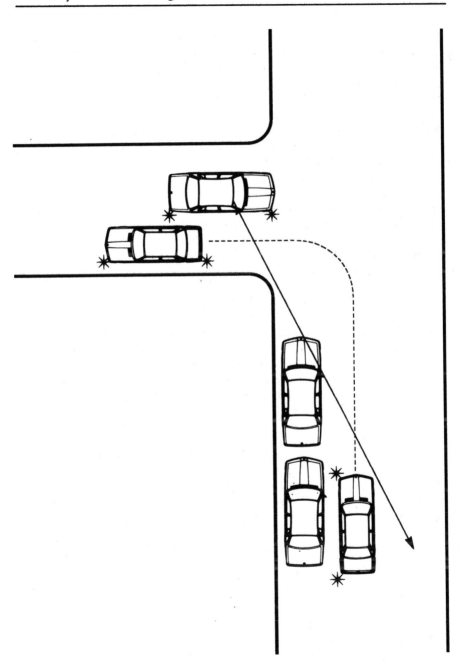

central position than normal, then the driver would need to pay particular attention to the possibility of his position suggesting that he was doing something other than turning left and, for example, a vehicle moving up along his near-side in the belief that the driver actually intended turning right.

Great care should be exercised by a driver if he ever finds it necessary to complete a manoeuvre from a lane which is specifically designated by signs and/or road markings for a manoeuvre other than his, and to do this is a decision which should not be made lightly. Where specific lanes are allocated to particular manoeuvres it is for reasons of traffic flow, and separating flows which may be a danger to each other. In addition, driving into a lane marked for turning left, for instance, is possibly the largest hint it is possible to give to other road users that that is in fact what the vehicle will be doing. To do anything other than turn left from that lane could be disastrous.

The above principles apply to all manoeuvres and at all times. There may, in addition to these, be more localized considerations relevant to the particular turn being made, or the particular vehicle being driven, or the particular route chosen. These too may, in certain circumstances, take on an importance which convinces the driver of the need to perform a given manoeuvre, or simply drive along, from a position other than the one that he otherwise would have chosen. The following are examples of such localized considerations:

❑ A move slightly to the left or right by the driver may put the wheels of his vehicle on a better or poorer quality road surface;

❑ A move to the left or right may, if the vehicle being driven is a large one, make a particular turn less or more severe, and therefore more or less manageable;

❑ Adopting a particular position may make a later manoeuvre less or more straightforward, e.g. following the road ahead from the right-hand lane at the first junction, in preparation for a right turn at the second.

As above, when adopting positions other than conventional ones, care must be taken as to the reactions induced in other road users.

By following the road ahead from the right-hand lane at the first junction, turning right at the seccond junction is made easier.

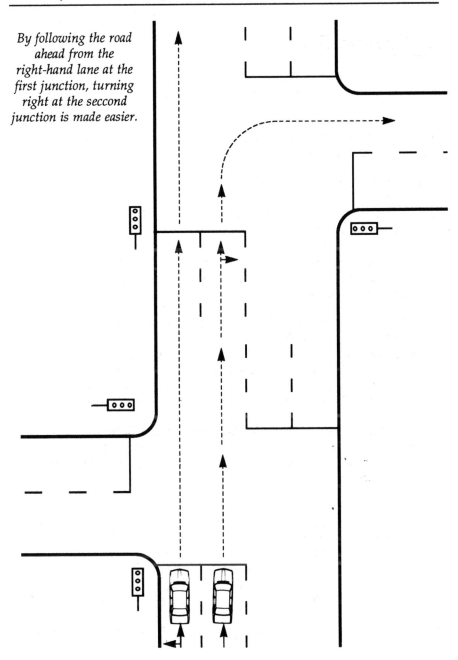

Following Position

Where there is no intention on the part of a driver to overtake the vehicle ahead, his aim should be to adopt a safe following position.

As a general principle, the more space which a driver keeps between his vehicle and the one ahead, the greater is his margin of safety in relation to dangers emanating from that leading vehicle.

The only safe rule is for a driver never to get closer to the vehicle ahead than the minimum distance he requires to stop his vehicle at his current speed and under the current conditions. The stopping distances listed in the Highway Code, and reproduced below, are based on a driver reaction time of 0.7 second, and assume that the vehicle is in good condition and travelling along a dry road. Should the driver's reaction time be extended for any reason, or should the road or vehicle conditions be unfavourable, then even more distance would be required.

It is sometimes suggested that at speeds of 40 mph and above, with all the conditions favourable as described above, a two second time gap between vehicles is sufficient. A two second time gap provides a driver with a gap which is approximately equivalent in yards to his speed in miles per hour, i.e. a two second time gap at 50 mph provides a gap of approximately 50 yards, and at 70 mph one of about 70 yards.

When the table below is examined, however, it will be seen that as the speed increases, so there is an increasing discrepancy between the gap being maintained and the distance which the driver requires to bring his vehicle to a stop.

speed (mph)	Two second time gap (feet)	(m)	Minimum stopping distance (feet)	(m)
40	117	36	120	36
50	147	45	175	53
60	176	54	240	73
70	205	62	315	96

Thus, whereas a driver travelling at 40 mph and maintaining a two second time gap virtually has his minimum stopping distance in front of

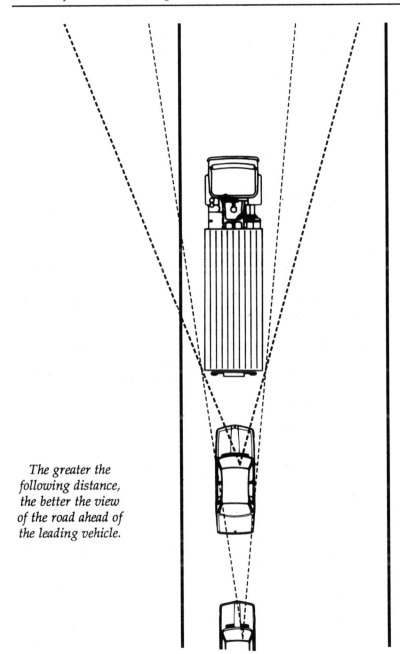

The greater the following distance, the better the view of the road ahead of the leading vehicle.

him, a driver travelling at 70 mph and maintaining the same time gap is 110 feet (34m) short of the distance he requires to stop his vehicle.

The argument which suggests that the reduced gap afforded by the two second time gap will be sufficient because the vehicle ahead will also have to slow down gradually is quickly and easily countered when it is realized that a vehicle ploughing into an immovable object such as a tree, bridge stanchion, or indeed an accident which already happened ahead of it, will not take any distance to gradually slow down, but rather will stop dead. Until a driver has seen the brake lights on the vehicle ahead light up he dare not assume that they are working, and that he will therefore be warned of the driver ahead slowing down suddenly.

Thus, a driver should at all times maintain at the very least a distance from the vehicle ahead equivalent to that required to stop his vehicle on that road at that speed. In addition to ensuring that he is able to stop in time should an incident occur ahead, a driver maintaining this gap will experience the following benefits:

❑ He will increase his view of the road ahead of the leading vehicle and therefore his awareness of the changing situation. This view may be increased still further by slight deviations to the near or off-sides.

❑ He will be able to produce a very economical and smooth drive as many situations encountered are dealt with simply by deceleration, rather than recourse to the brake pedal.

❑ He will be able to extend the braking distance of a vehicle following too close to him by slowing his own vehicle down gradually over a long distance.

Whilst all three of these benefits are of importance to the advanced driver the advantages produced by the first two points above are the ones most commonly utilized. The advanced driver may easily be compared and contrasted with the one not so advanced, as the latter adopts a position close to the vehicle ahead of him and then is required to dance repeatedly between the accelerator and brake pedals in response to fluctuations in speed from the leading vehicle, which in turn are caused by changes in road conditions ahead which of course the non-advanced driver cannot see.

Overtaking Position

The overtaking position differs from the following position in that the former is generally closer to the vehicle ahead than the latter. It is close enough to allow for the manoeuvre, once begun, to be completed in the minimum amount of time, but not so close that the checks of the road ahead which need to be made before its commencement are not possible.

The degree to which the overtaking position is closer than the following position will depend upon the speed of the vehicles concerned, and by how much the speed of the overtaking vehicle will exceed that of the target vehicle. If the overtaking vehicle will reach a speed well in excess of that of the target vehicle then, for a given view ahead, its driver may begin the manoeuvre from a greater distance than the one whose vehicle will achieve a speed less in excess of that of the target vehicle.

If the overtaking position is significantly closer to the target vehicle than what would, under those circumstances, be a safe following distance then it should be the overtaking driver's aim to spend as little time there as possible. Once the possibility of an overtake has been sighted and initial checks of the road ahead are encouraging, then the driver should move up to the overtaking position.

Depending on the particular circumstances, it may or may not be necessary to carry out the checks of the road ahead again, but very quickly the driver should now decide whether he is or is not going to perform the overtake. If he decides he is, then he should do so; if not, then he should drop back to his following position and await another opportunity.

Positioning for Bends

The fundamental rule of positioning, that is, that the driver occupies whichever is the safest place on the road at any given moment in time, applies as much to his approach to bends as any other situation. The view around a right-hand bend may often be maximized by the driver positioning his vehicle well into the left of the road. This is often the safest place for him to be, and therefore the correct place, because the earlier he sights a potential hazard the more time be will have in which to deal with it.

When that potential hazard is an oncoming vehicle, then the earlier the two drivers are able to see each other the more likely it is that they will pass safely. However, examples of factors arguing against a position change to the left on the approach to a right-hand bend would be:

❏ A poor quality road surface towards the edge of the road;

❏ The presence of pedestrians close to the road;

❏ The existence of blind side roads/driveways on the left edge of the road.

If these disadvantages outweigh the advantage of an earlier and further view around the bend then a position well into the left would not be adopted.

On the approach to a left-band bend the driver's view of the road ahead may often be maximized by positioning his vehicle towards the centre of-the road. In determining whether this is the correct place for him to be he must balance the advantages gained in terms of view and warning of hazards ahead against the possible disadvantages emanating from the fact that his vehicle, as it stands, is now closer to the path of an oncoming vehicle, and especially those which may cut across the apex of the bend.

Provided the driver has sufficient time to regain the left side of the road if this proves to be necessary, then this is not a problem, but in urban areas, at relatively low speeds, this disadvantage, together with the fact that, as discussed, a position towards the centre of the road may mislead following traffic as to his real intentions, often convinces a driver to approach a left-hand bend from a more conventional position on the road. Likewise, on a very narrow country lane a left-hand bend would probably be approached from a position even more to the left than usual because of the very short period of time which would be available for regaining the left once an oncoming vehicle was sighted.

The improvement in forward vision resulting from the above suggested positioning on the approach to bends is not the only advantage which the driver experiences. By positioning well into the left of the road on the approach to a right-hand bend, and towards the centre of the road on the approach to a left-hand bend, the driver may give himself the opportunity of finding a curved path of larger radius within the bend than the radius of the bend itself. As seen in Chapter 4, 'Braking, Gear Changing, Accelerating and Steering', it should be the driver's aim at all times to make the most gradual change possible to the direction of his vehicle. By doing so the risk of its being fatally destabilized is minimized.

A line of greater radius than the bend itself through a right-hand bend may be found by positioning well to the left of the road on the approach, moving on a curved path towards the centre of the road once the view around the bend has opened up, and then easing his vehicle back towards the near-side of the road as he exits the bend.

Having entered a left-hand bend from a position towards the centre of the road a curved path towards the left edge of the road once the view around the bend has opened up may provide the driver with a curved path of greater radius and therefore greater stability. Whether it does so will depend mainly upon how early the view around the bend opens up.

It must be emphasized that these routes through bends are only followed if, in all the circumstances prevailing at the time, and when all the advantages and disadvantages have been duly weighed, they are considered to be the safest routes.

6

Observation and Anticipation

or

"Seek and ye shall find"

A driver's primary requirement as he progresses along the road is information. That is, information about what is happening and what is going to happen. Clearly, if the driver knew both of these things the whole of the time, then the driving task would instantly become very straightforward and almost perfectly safe.

Examples of typical questions a driver would like answering in the course of a journey include:

❑ How sharp is the next bend?

❑ What is around the next bend?

❑ Is that driver going to wait until I have gone past before emerging from that junction?

❑ Is anything going to cause that cyclist to wobble in the next few seconds?

❑ Are there any children playing behind that parked car?

❑ Will those traffic lights change colour before I arrive there?

❑ Where is the school to which that sign refers?

It may now be seen why local knowledge is of such importance to a driver. If a driver is familiar with a road he will know the answer to the first two, and last questions above, and will probably be able to make a fair guess about the traffic lights.

Local knowledge will not, however, assist him with the remaining questions, and consequently drivers must realize that no matter how familiar they are with a particular stretch of road their full attention is required to address these and other similar questions.

Any questions which a driver may not answer with certainty, and that will include any question involving the future movements of other road users, he is reduced to taking his best guess at, or, in other words, anticipating the answer to. In order to anticipate, however, he must first observe.

Observation

Observation whilst driving should be a positive, rather than a passive activity. A driver should not be satisfied with seeing; rather, he should *seek*. He should actively seek out information, as opposed to passively noting things which present themselves in front of him. There is a vast amount of information available to a driver should he wish to find it.

A driver's eyes should be making constant sweeps of all the space which he can see from his vehicle. He should focus on objects and situations as far ahead as possible, and then work back to the middle and then the near distances. By the time all the available information from these points of focus has been collected and sifted, his vehicle will have moved further along the road and the process will need to be begun again.

Interspersed with this forward observation should be checks to the left and the right, and, as mentioned elsewhere, the rear.

The existence of blind spots, that is, areas around his vehicle which he cannot see into, caused either by the bodywork of his vehicle obscuring a certain area, or simply by the inability of the vehicle's mirrors to reveal the whole of the space behind and to the sides, should be borne in mind at all times by the driver. When talking in terms of all round observation these areas too need checking.

Driving along involves a constant process of sweeping the whole of the area around a vehicle. If anything of particular note is sighted, or any movement picked up by peripheral vision, then the driver's attention may be focused on it and the problem solving procedure begun if necessary.

Many drivers are surprised at precisely how far ahead they are able to see once they actually look, and of the benefit of so doing. It is a natural human trait to focus one's attention, whatever the activity, only a short distance ahead ('short' being relative to the speed). The proportion of people who may be seen walking through beautiful countryside looking only two or three paces ahead of themselves, as if searching for dropped money, bears testament to this.

But an advanced driver cannot afford to satisfy himself with this amount of forward observation. He requires earlier and more plentiful information than this behaviour brings, and therefore he raises his eyes and casts them as far down the road as possible. It must be remembered, forewarned is forearmed.

A non-advanced driver, on checking his mirrors in preparation for moving out to the right to pass the next stationary vehicle, will often see that the advanced driver behind has already moved out and taken up position in the right-hand lane. By looking further ahead the advanced driver was able to plan and act earlier.

Again, one of the hallmarks of the advanced driver is that he will often begin reducing speed for the next hazard earlier than the vehicle ahead. The brake lights of the advanced driver will often be seen to light up before those on the vehicle in front, even though it is the leading one which is actually going to reach the hazard first. The reason for this is that the advanced driver has looked further ahead than the one not so advanced. Earlier information means earlier action. Earlier action generally results in a smoother and more controlled response to the hazard.

Even information which is not directly useful at the moment it is gathered should be filed away for future reference, when it may become useful. For instance, consider the driver who identifies a set of traffic lights three quarters of a mile ahead. At 30 mph it will take him one and a half minutes to reach them. Their present colour does not affect him, but, if he checked their colour every, say, 10 seconds he may be able to acquire sufficient information about those lights to enable him to predict what their colour will be when be does reach them.

The effect on observation of driving at high speeds must be understood by drivers. As the speed of his vehicle increases so, quite naturally and unintentionally, does the driver focus further along the road. This is clearly desirable in view of the fact that he is reaching points along the road in a shorter time, but it is undesirable in that near distance details become incomplete and intermittent and information is missed. Peripheral vision does not fill in the minute details. A good demonstration of this effect is seen when a person stands away from, and scours a crowd of people for a particular individual. As they focus in the distance on the members of the crowd it is possible for the person they seek to approach them from the front or side unnoticed.

Thus, in busy situations drivers must moderate their speeds. This is to ensure not only that they are able to stop within the distance they can see to be clear, a basic rule of driving, but also that they allow themselves time and opportunity to observe all the relevant detail. The road ahead may be clear for 60 yards, suggesting a safe speed of 50 mph, but a clue on the right or left may suggest that it is about to cease to be clear.

As regards eyesight, the present legal requirement is for a driver to be able to read a number plate with $3^1/_8''$ characters at 67 feet, or one with $3^1/_2''$ characters at 75 feet, in good daylight, with spectacles or contact lenses, if worn. This is not a particularly demanding standard, especially when it is realized that approximately 80% of a driver's information comes via his or her eyes. It goes without saying that all windows in the vehicle should be as clean as possible; that windscreen wipers should be in good working order; and that water should always be available in the windscreen washer bottle.

Commentary driving

The subject of concentration is closely allied to that of observation. A driver who is not concentrating fully is a driver who is not observing fully. The possible reasons for the lack of total concentration (and the average driver is able to concentrate fully on any activity, including the driving task, to the exclusion of all other matters only for about 20 minutes; after that time the level of concentration falls gradually away to a trough before picking up again) are numerous. Fatigue, ill health, stress and anger are just a few of them. If the driver is aware at any stage that his concentration is anything but total, then he should reduce his speed to one commensurate with the level of concentration he is able to apply.

A great aid to concentration is commentary driving: the driver talks aloud about what he is doing with his vehicle, and why. Although many drivers are a little uncomfortable or embarrassed when they provide a commentary for the first time, and find it difficult not to think more about what they are saying than what they are doing, these feelings should be overcome when it is realized that to provide a commentary is simply to say aloud the thoughts which should be going through the driver's mind anyway.

The commentary as an aid to concentration works on the principle that it is virtually impossible for a human being to talk sensibly about one subject while thinking about another. Thus, if the driver talks coherently and sensibly about the driving task, as he performs it, this will ensure that he is concentrating on it to his full potential. Also, doing so will encourage him to get his eyes ranging far and wide as he seeks out items upon which to comment.

Providing a commentary over any period of time proves tiring – another testament to the fact that doing so is requiring the driver's brain to work hard. It can also take its toll of the vocal chords. Advanced drivers do not commentate the whole time that they are driving. Rather, they recognize the benefits of a commentary and will use it to drag their level of concentration back to that required whenever they feel it slipping.

A good commentary will always be based on the present and future tenses, rather than the past tense. A passenger listening to a driver giving a commentary would be referred to situations ahead of the vehicle which have yet to be dealt with, rather than those behind which have already been dealt with. He would be informed of what the driver is doing, or is going to do, rather than what he has already done. Thus, providing a commentary of high standard demands of the driver good observation allied with good forward planning – two further factors which will assist the quality and safety of his drive.

Driving plans and zones of invisibility

A driving plan, that is, the solution the driver develops to solve the problem which he has identified, is based on a combination of three factors:

❏ What he can see;

❏ What he cannot see, and

❏ Circumstances which he may reasonably expect to develop.

(The third point will be dealt with fully under 'Anticipation'.)

The areas around his vehicle which a driver is unable to see into, the 'zones of invisibility', are clearly just as important to him as the areas into which he can see. Where they exist the driver must assume the worst about that space and develop a plan which will deal with it should the assumption prove to be correct. Thus, for instance, unless the driver is able to check and see for certain, it must be assumed that behind every parked vehicle is a child ready to run into the road. He would then need to position his vehicle, and drive it at such a speed, that if this working assumption is indeed correct he would be able to deal with the situation safely. If the assumption proves to be incorrect, and there is no child, then the driver has lost nothing. He should prepare for the worst, and then rejoice if it does not materialize.

The number of 'zones of invisibility' experienced by the advanced driver will be fewer than those experienced by the non-advanced driver because the former will recognize the benefits of, amongst others, the following matters:

❑ Reflections in shop windows to see around a corner or bend, or further along a queue of traffic;

The observant driver would be aware of the approach of the car reflected in the facing shop window.

❑ Gaps, albeit small ones, in walls or hedges which provide fleeting glimpses of the road ahead or into side roads;

❑ The space underneath a stationary vehicle through which pedestrians' feet may often be sighted;

❑ The ceilings of buses for warning of traffic movement further along a stationary queue;

The tailgate up on the parked vehicle suggests the presence of at least one pedestrian. The advanced driver uses the space underneath the vehicle to locate one.

❑ The line taken by street lamps on the far side of a hump-backed bridge for indication of the route followed by the road.

The topic of zones of invisibility is closely connected to that of positioning. Not only does the advanced driver recognize that there are numerous aids to seeing into apparently blind areas, but he also realizes that often even small changes to the position of his vehicle an the road will open up areas to him which were previously obscured. Two of the more common examples of this would be:

❑ By coming to a stop in a line of traffic slightly to the right of the vehicle ahead, rather than directly behind it, an improved view of the road ahead will result in earlier warning of a likely move off.

❑ By moving out towards the centre of the road an improved view into the area behind a parked vehicle will be gained.

Providing these small position changes do not lead to confusion in the minds of other road users, and this matter is discussed more fully in Chapter 5, 'Positioning', they are both legitimate and advisable.

To the driver who wishes to know the probable direction of the road over the brow of the hill, the street lamps are shouting out!

As regards matters observed, it is often the smallest detail which gives the largest clue about what is happening or is likely to happen. The non-advanced driver would notice only the Pelican crossing ahead. The advanced driver would go a stage further and observe that the pedestrian 'wait' sign had been illuminated. The non-advanced driver would notice only the bus stationary at a bus stop ahead. The advanced driver would go further and observe that the last passenger to board had finished paying his fare and was moving down the bus.

Once the clue has been observed, it must then be interpreted.

Anticipation

This is the ability of a driver to predict the likely outcome of a given situation on the basis of what he has observed. It is based on imagination, common sense and experience, and when raised to a high level of skill, allows the driver to remove from almost all of the situations which he encounters the 'element of surprise'.

Once a driver has observed a hazardous or potentially hazardous situation developing he then attempts to anticipate its outcome. If he is able to do so he is clearly in a much better position from which to plan his own movements than if he is unable to do so.

He attempts to anticipate the outcome using a process of constant cross referencing of the present situation, or details from it, with similar ones which he has encountered in the past. For instance, if on previous occasions the driver bas noticed that cyclists, shortly after looking over their right shoulders, often move out to the right, when he then finds himself behind a rider who does this he may anticipate that this cyclist will also shortly move out to the right. If the driver has anticipated the situation correctly he will ensure that he and his vehicle are in such a position as to be able to deal safely with the movement from the rider.

Again, if experience has taught a driver that a common occurrence near to motorway slip roads is for drivers to make late lane changes in order to take those slip roads, when he is next travelling along a motorway and approaching an exit he will be especially wary of such drivers.

It is sometimes the small details which the driver is able to compare with previous experiences. For example, if a driver has experienced the reluctance of a cold engine to accelerate smartly on occasions, when be next observes an excessive amount of exhaust emanating from a vehicle on a winter's morning, he should be ready for that apparently recently started vehicle to dawdle when moving off from its next stop.

This technique of cross referencing with past experiences does, to some degree, categorize people. Experienced drivers will often be more wary of a young driver in a sporty type car than an older man who has his wife and children as passengers in what might be termed a family estate. This is not to suggest that all young males driving sporty cars behave recklessly, but experience may suggest that a larger proportion of them do than of the other type of driver.

Another technique which may be usefully employed when attempting to predict the behaviour of other road users is for the driver to ask himself: "If I were that other road user, what would I do in that situation?". For instance, if a driver is wondering whether another driver waiting at a junction on the left will emerge before or after he passes that road, he should ask himself whether he would emerge in that gap if it were him waiting at the junction. If he feels that there would be sufficient time for him to emerge safely then a good working assumption would probably be that the other driver will consider that there is sufficient time also.

There must always, of course, be built into the driving plan which a driver develops on the basis of his anticipation the possibility that he has assessed the situation incorrectly, and that something entirely different may occur. In the example just given, for instance, the driver waiting at the junction may, for whatever reason, arrive at precisely the opposite conclusion about what is or is not a safe gap. Again, although it is much less common for elderly pedestrians to make sudden, unexpected darts across the road than it is for young children, any driving plan formulated to deal with a group of elderly pedestrians must take into account the possibility of this happening.

Observation links

In the pursuit of information about what is or is not likely to happen the use of observation links is invaluable. A driver makes an observation link when he observes one thing and from it deduces another. The examples of the cyclist who glances over his right shoulder before moving out, and the behaviour of drivers near to motorway exits given earlier constitute observation links.

There is an observation link to be made in almost every detail which a driver may notice, should he care to take the trouble and find it. If the driver works on the basis that there is a reason for everything, and that if that reason can be found his understanding of, and ability to deal safely with, the situation in question will be greatly increased, he will not be far wrong.

An enquiring mind is one of the advanced driver's most valuable attributes. The technique of observing a situation and then responding in his own mind with a sentence beginning either *"Who...... ?"*, *"What..... ?"*, *"Where......?"*, *"When......?"*, *"Why.......?"* or *"How.......?"* is fundamental to his ability to drive along in a progressive but unhurried manner, and to be in a position to respond satisfactorily to everything which occurs.

The following are examples of some common observation links:

❏ The pedestrian 'wait' sign at a Pelican crossing is illuminated. The lights are due to change from green.

❏ The last boarding passenger is moving down the bus. The driver will wish to move away soon.

❏ Oncoming vehicles have headlights switched on during daylight. The driver is approaching bad weather.

❏ A football is bouncing into the road from a driveway. A child may run out to collect it.

❏ The vehicle ahead is stopping on the left. The driver's door may open.

❏ Driving in the vicinity of a hospital. In addition to emergency vehicles there may be drivers in the locality preoccupied with thoughts of sick relatives etc.

❏ A sign ahead marking a change in Local Authority. The nature of the road surface will change also.

The road surface changes at the county boundary. Notice also the change in the barrier and the lack of any Vibroline rumble strip in this part of Derbyshire.

A driver can justifiably claim to display good anticipation only when the stage is reached where he is very rarely, if ever, taken by surprise by anything during his journeys. To an interested observer seated alongside him his vehicle would appear to flow along the road, with the driver seeming to deal with situations almost before they occurred. Very rarely would anything more severe than a gentle amount of braking, or steering, or acceleration be required. To the interested, non-driving observer the driving task would appear to be very straightforward, and each journey made with this driver would be memorable only for the fact that nothing appeared to happen.

7

Overtaking

or

"He who hesitates is lost"

It is a curious fact that whilst, of all the common driving manoeuvres, it is the one of overtaking a moving vehicle which is potentially the most dangerous, this is also the skill in which the driver is least likely to have received any specific instruction while he was being taught how to drive. The reasons for this are that for novice drivers, the opportunity to carry out an overtake does not occur very frequently (particularly on single carriageway roads) due to that driver's generally relatively low speeds, and that for the instructor it is virtually impossible to plan such a manoeuvre prior to a lesson.

Thus, most drivers acquire their overtaking technique over a period of time once they have passed their 'L' test, and on a trial and error basis. What worked the first time will probably be repeated, until such time as a situation arises which the driver finds uncomfortable. He will then either modify his technique in an attempt to eliminate the problem which had arisen, or, at least equally likely, he will assume that the problem could not be eliminated by any change in his behaviour, and so will continue using the same technique in future.

However, as with all other aspects of driving, there is a correct way in which to carry out the manoeuvre and there are many incorrect ways. By overtaking in the correct fashion the driver reduces to a minimum the risks involved with the exercise, and increases to a maximum his safety margins at all stages while it is being carried out.

It should be understood that providing the vehicle ahead is moving in the same direction, albeit very slowly, it is not strictly speaking necessary for a following driver to overtake it in order for him to reach his destination. Only when the vehicle ahead is stationary does an overtake become a necessity.

It is often suggested that the first question a driver should ask of himself when considering overtaking the vehicle ahead is *"Is it necessary?"*. In terms of actually reaching the end of his journey the answer to this question is always going to be *"No, it is not"*. Furthermore, given that an overtake should only ever be carried out if, during the manoeuvre itself, the same quality of safety may be maintained as at all other times, then there should never be an answer to the above question which runs along the following lines: *"Although I recognize that this is not an ideal situation in. which to carry out an overtake, I am going to do so anyway because there is an overriding consideration which renders it necessary that I do"*. If it is safe and lawful, an overtake may be carried out. If it is not, then one should not be – irrespective of whether it is 'necessary' or not. Whether the reason given is an apparent saving in journey time, or to assist clearing a backlog of traffic building up behind a slow moving vehicle, there is no reason a driver can give which is sufficiently 'necessary' to justify compromising his own and other road users' safety.

Thus, the decision to overtake is based upon considerations other than necessity. Given that it is safe and lawful and not inconvenient to other road users to do so, a driver decides either that he will or will not perform the manoeuvre in precisely the same way as he decides whether he will or will not turn left into the next side road; or whether he will take the first or second exit from the next roundabout; or whether he will stop at this petrol station or one further along the road. A more useful first question for a driver to ask when gaining on a slower moving vehicle, rather than *"Is it necessary?"* would be *"Given all the circumstances prevailing at the moment, does it suit my personal situation more to overtake this vehicle, or to pull in behind and follow it?"*

The success or otherwise of an overtaking manoeuvre depends essentially upon the ability of the overtaking driver to ensure two things.

Firstly, he must ensure that the road ahead is clear and that it will remain so long enough for him to move out, pass the 'target' vehicle, and then return to the left.

Secondly, he needs to ensure that the target vehicle will remain on a steady course for as long as the manoeuvre takes, and especially that it will not deviate significantly to the right.

The first of these criteria is more easily guaranteed on dual rather than single carriageway type roads, because here the probability of any intrusion from the off-side, either by oncoming vehicles or by other road users emerging from junctions etc. is virtually eliminated. For this reason it is the more difficult technique of overtaking safely on a single carriageway road which will be referred to most often in this discussion, although many of the points made will also be relevant to the manoeuvre carried out on a dual carriageway.

The two criteria mentioned above will now be examined in turn.

The road ahead must be, and remain, clear

❏ The length of road required.

> The length of road which the overtaking driver needs to ensure is, and will remain, clear will vary between overtakes. It will depend upon the following three factors:
>
> ✓ The speed of the vehicle to be overtaken;
>
> ✓ The speed of his own vehicle;
>
> ✓ The performance of his own vehicle.
>
> The driver who is wishing to overtake a target vehicle which is travelling close to the maximum speed which his own vehicle will attain during the manoeuvre will require more time and therefore (relatively) more road than the driver whose vehicle will attain a much higher speed than that of the target vehicle.

As an example, if an overtaking vehicle maintains a speed which is 10 mph faster than that of a target vehicle, 'approximately 12 seconds will elapse between the overtaking vehicle moving from a position 30 yards behind the target vehicle to one of 30 yards in front of it. If the speed differential is 30 mph, however, only about 4 seconds will elapse between these two points. With the target vehicle travelling at, say, 40 mph, this would mean the difference between the overtaking driver requiring 1,576 feet (480m) of clear road, or only 642 feet (196m).

In practice the road ahead will need to be seen to be clear for a greater distance even than this, in order to allow for the approach of oncoming vehicles either seen or as yet unseen. Two vehicles travelling towards each other at 60 mph (i.e. a closing speed of 120 mph) are closing at 176 feet/sec. (54m/sec.). Thus, with a target vehicle travelling at 40 mph, an overtaking vehicle travelling at 60 mph and an oncoming vehicle approaching at 60 mph, in order to complete the manoeuvre safely the overtaking driver will need approximately 1,404 feet (428m) between himself and the approaching vehicle when commencing the manoeuvre.

Furthermore, the performance rather than simply the top speed of the overtaking driver's vehicle is relevant because in many instances the length of road required for completion of the manoeuvre will be minimized where the overtaking vehicle is capable of reaching a satisfactory speed differential with the target vehicle in a short period of time. Generally speaking, the better the performance of the overtaking driver's vehicle, the more efficiently and briskly he will be able to complete the manoeuvre.

❑ Checking the road ahead.

As a general rule, the closer a driver puts his vehicle to the one ahead of him, the less of the road in front of the leading vehicle he will be able to see. This is especially true where the leading vehicle is high-sided, such as a lorry or a bus. By moving up close the following driver may increase and improve his view *through* the leading vehicle, but the benefits from this position change are generally outweighed by the disadvantages emanating from the reduced view around it.

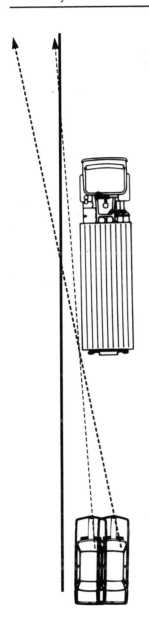

From a position well back from the target vehicle, then, the following position changes should be considered in order to view the road ahead of it.

Initially, the driver should consider moving his vehicle into the left-hand side of the road. By so doing he will increase the distance along the edge of the road on the near-side of the target vehicle that he is able to see compared with his previously more central following position. The further left of the target vehicle he is able to position himself the further along and ahead of it he will see. Precisely how far into the left he is able to go will be governed by the degree of danger he perceives as being present on that side of the road. For instance, if along the left-hand side of the road in question was a series of concealed entrances that driver could not safely move over as far as the driver who was travelling along a road with 20 yards of grass verge between it and the entrances.

By moving to the left, the driver may be able to see further along the nearside of the target vehicle.

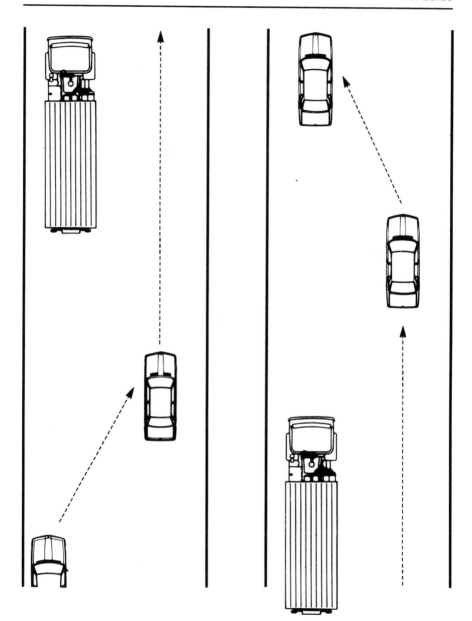

Having carried out this check along the near-side of the target vehicle, if the driver considers that an overtake is still a possibility he now needs to set about checking the area of road directly in front of it. This is best done by moving out onto the passing line well before drawing up alongside the target vehicle. If an overtake along a straight stretch of road is taken as an example, by moving out early and travelling along a line parallel to that of the target vehicle the area of road directly ahead of the latter will gradually and progressively become visible to the overtaking driver as he closes on it. The point is eventually reached where the information provided by this position change, together with that which was provided by the earlier move to the left, means that all areas of road should now be accounted for.

Failing to move out far enough, early enough, is the most common, and potentially dangerous, flaw in the overtaking technique of most drivers. They are prepared to adopt a position on the right-hand side of the road only momentarily before drawing up along-side the rear bumper of their target vehicle, and then, because they have drawn up so close behind it, when they do achieve the right-hand side of

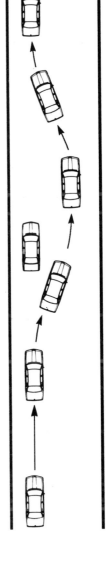

By swooping out from behind the target vehicle in this fashion, forward vision is reduced and safety margins are minimised.

the road they do so at an angle to the target vehicle, rather than parallel to it. By closing up on the target vehicle and then swooping out at this angle from behind it a driver experiences the following disadvantages compared to the one who moves out much earlier and approaches on a parallel course:

✓ Because he only obtains a satisfactory view of the road ahead of the target vehicle once he has begun drawing up alongside it, if he were to see anything to suggest that an overtake should not now be completed he must severely reduce speed and turn his vehicle through a sharp angle to the left before being able to drop back in behind it. The driver who performs the manoeuvre correctly, as described above, will sight the problem before reaching the point where he is alongside the target vehicle, and when he is travelling parallel to it, and he is able then to simply 'drift' his vehicle back in to the left to drop in behind it.

✓ He reveals himself and his intentions to the driver of the target vehicle at a later stage in the manoeuvre.

✓ He reveals himself and his intentions to drivers of oncoming vehicles at a later stage in the manoeuvre.

Bends in the road may be used to advantage when attempting to check the road ahead of the target vehicle. When approaching a left-hand bend, by moving his vehicle out towards the centre of the road the following driver will achieve an extended view along the near-side of the target vehicle and ahead of it. On the approach to a right-hand bend by moving in towards the left the following driver achieves an improved view along the off-side of the target vehicle and further along the road. In order to maximize these advantages it is, depending upon the severity of the bend, legitimate to consider moving up closer to the target vehicle than generally recommended, with the proviso that only the minimum amount of time is spent in this position. Once there and the view has been obtained, then the driver should be immediately considering doing one of two things: either commencing the overtake or dropping back to a safer following position.

The following are examples of circumstances and situations which the driver considering an overtake may view from either of these position changes which suggest to him that the road ahead is not clear, or will not remain clear for a sufficient length of time:

✓ Oncoming vehicles;

✓ A side road/lay-by entrance to either the left or right from which other road users may emerge;

✓ A bend/hill crest around or over which other road users may appear.

✓ Pedestrians, especially children, near to the road way.

There is unquestionably only one safe maxim: If in any doubt, do not overtake.

When considering an overtake the driver dare not concentrate his attention solely on the situation ahead. If he too has following traffic he must be aware of the possibility of one of these drivers commencing an overtake of his vehicle. The consequences of his moving out to the right at the same moment as be himself is being overtaken are fairly obvious.

Also, when considering when, and by how much, to make a position change to the left and right in order to view the road ahead he must be aware of the possibility of the following driver moving up and taking the space which his vehicle has just vacated. This is especially pertinent when planning the move out to the right, because it is possible that in the event of his having to abort the overtake and move back in to the left, if the following driver does move up there will be no space to move back in to. If these appear to be credible dangers, then the driver should not attempt an overtake.

The target vehicle must remain on a steady course

In the course of a normal overtake on a single carriageway road reasons for the target vehicle to deviate unexpectedly to the left are few, and if such a situation did occur it would not necessarily be dangerous. More likely, and potentially disastrous, is an unexpected deviation to the right. Measures must be taken by the overtaking driver to reduce this risk to a minimum.

The following are examples of situations which the overtaking driver may observe ahead of the target vehicle which would suggest that precisely this is likely to happen, and that consequently an overtake should not be attempted.

❑ A stationary obstruction, e.g. parked vehicles or roadworks around which the driver ahead may deviate;

❑ An even slower moving vehicle, e.g. a cyclist which he may move out to overtake;

❑ A side road/lay-by/entrance to either the left or right into which the driver ahead may turn, or which may result in his swerving to the right in order to avoid another emerging driver;

❑ A break in the building line resulting in a gust of wind blowing him off course to the right;

❑ A pot-hole in the road which he may decide to drive around.

However, even given that no circumstances such as these are observed, it is still desirable that the driver of the target vehicle is aware of the presence and intentions of the driver wishing to overtake him. If he is so aware it is less likely that he himself will adopt any behaviour during the time that the manoeuvre takes which would endanger either party.

The most obvious means by which the driver of the target vehicle may be alerted as to the presence of the overtaking driver is by use of the horn. The note should be firm and positive without being aggressive, and should be given from a sufficient distance that if any undesirable reaction is provoked in the leading driver, it will not cause a problem to the overtaking driver.

The presence of background noise, for instance when overtaking a vehicle moving at speed or when that vehicle is either open (e.g. a tractor) or intrinsically noisy (e.g. a lorry), means that often a more reliable method of indicating his presence would be for the overtaking driver to flash his headlamps. Care must be taken when using this signal, however, due to the numerous different interpretations given to it by drivers.

If there is any likelihood of the driver of the target vehicle misunderstanding the headlamp flash as meaning that he is being given room to pull out himself, possibly to carry out an overtake, then the signal should not be used.

Consideration must be given to applying a right-hand indicator prior to commencing the overtaking manoeuvre. Its purpose would be to warn other road users, including possibly the driver of the target vehicle, of the intention to move to the right, but it should never be used in an attempt to create a gap which does not exist.

When the situation is arrived at where the area of road ahead of the target vehicle has been checked, and the overtaking driver is happy that, if necessary, the driver of the target vehicle has been warned of his presence, then the overtaking driver should aim to complete the manoeuvre as briskly as possible. The period of time during which he is alongside the target vehicle is generally the one during which he is exposed to most danger, and the aim should be to keep this time to a minimum. When the overtaking driver has decided to go, then that is precisely what he should do – and go quickly. When overtaking there is more than just an element of truth in the maxim *"He who hesitates is lost"*.

If any gear change is necessary it should be made before moving up alongside the target vehicle. To make a gear change while actually alongside it brings the following disadvantages.

❏ The driver has one hand away from the steering wheel during the critical period, and

❏ There would probably be a momentary loss in momentum of the vehicle as the clutch is depressed, which results in the manoeuvre taking longer than necessary.

During the manoeuvre the overtaking driver must continue to observe the scene ahead for any change in circumstances, but it may also be useful for him to glance into the off-side door or wing mirror of the target vehicle in order that the state of its driver may be observed. If it is noticed that he is occupied with matters other than the overtake which is being attempted consideration may be given to aborting the manoeuvre.

If the procedure as described above is carried out, it will be seen that there are no changes in state of the overtaking driver's vehicle which are fierce. All alterations of position, direction, and speed are carried out smoothly and in accordance with the principles of motion described elsewhere in this book.

Although sometimes a driver needs to respond quickly in order to take advantage of an opportunity that has arisen for carrying out an overtake, there is a world of difference between this, acting quickly but correctly, and simply 'snatching' at the speed and direction of a vehicle in order to carry out the operation.

The advanced driver follows a logical sequence of thoughts and actions prior to overtaking albeit that he sometimes goes through them quickly. The non-advanced driver simply acts quickly, with no predetermined plan governing what he considers and what he does. It is small wonder, then, that with this most dangerous of all manoeuvres things sometimes go wrong.

Escape Routes

The advanced driver is continually aware of the possibility that at any given moment in time, either he or another road user may make a mistake in their driving. He recognizes that nobody is perfect.

With this in mind, he does not drive in such a way as to merely reduce to a minimum the number of mistakes made, but rather also their consequences should they occur.

With the best laid plans of mice and men occasionally going astray, whether it is while carrying out overtakes or at any other time, the advanced driver will have decided prior to actually commencing his overtake where his escape route will be should he find himself in need of one. He will not wait until the emergency has arisen before beginning to weigh up the relative advantages of, for instance, braking in a straight line, or deviating to the left onto a grass verge, or to the right into a lay-by; he will have done most of that thinking beforehand.

Thus, for example, when, in spite of his best efforts, the target vehicle does veer to the right at the crucial moment during the manoeuvre, the advanced driver will have planned for this contingency and ensured that he has an escape route available and he will be ready to make use of it. If there is not one available – if there would be nowhere to go should difficulties arise during the overtake – then the advanced driver would not begin the exercise.

He will not contemplate a manoeuvre, the thinking behind which runs as follows: *"As long as everything goes the way I expect and nothing untoward happens, I should be alright."*

The System of Car Control

or

"I came, I saw, I dealt with safely"

For the driver of a motor vehicle, every journey consists essentially of a series of hazards to be negotiated. Only if he succeeds in negotiating safely each and every one of the hazards he encounters in the course of a journey will the driver reach his destination unscathed. If he fails to negotiate any one of them, then he becomes involved in an incident.

The number of hazards met by a driver varies from journey to journey, and whilst it is often true that a longer distance travelled will involve more than a short one, this is not always the case. A relatively brief trip through a busy city centre may present a driver with numerically more problems than a longer drive along a quiet country road, for instance.

In the city centre, it would be a continuous and unrelenting sequence of situations to be dealt with, the driver no sooner resolving one before having another one presented in front of him. On occasions he may even be dealing with several at the same time. On the quiet country road there may be intervals of several seconds, or even longer, between individual hazards.

Furthermore, a given route will present a different number of hazards to the driver each time it is travelled. No two journeys are the same, even if they are the same journey. On one occasion, for instance, there may have been a group of children playing outside the shops; on the next there may not have been, but instead the driver may have found a young cyclist at the T-junction and a loose dog near the park.

Thus, familiarity with a particular route does not guarantee knowledge of the problems which will be encountered along it, and so, whilst local knowledge is of great assistance to a driver, the situation should never be reached where familiarity breads contempt, and the driver plans his drive solely on the basis of what has happened in the past. Simply because to date there have never been any vehicles approaching from the left when the driver has turned at a particular junction at a particular time, this does not guarantee that there will never be.

Some of the hazards along a given route are ever-present, and if a driver travels the route regularly he will be aware of them and should be prepared for them. Examples of this would include a bend, or the brow of a hill or a set of traffic lights.

The driver should realize, however, that the same hazard can present different problems depending on the time of day at which it is approached, or the day of the week, or the week of the year. The bend mentioned above may be an entirely different proposition when approached on a frosty December morning than when approached on a warm summer afternoon. Likewise, the brow of the hill would present more problems when the sun was shining over the brow directly into the eyes of the drivers ascending the hill, than it would at other times.

The most comprehensive and thorough problem solving procedure yet devised for a driver is the System of Car Control, and this will now be examined. It will be seen to be very logical, essentially simple and the embodiment of good driving practices.

The System of Car Control

The System of Car Control (otherwise known simply as "The System") was devised in 1937 at the Metropolitan Police Driving School at Hendon.

The school itself had been established three years prior to that, in 1934, in an attempt to improve the standard of training given to police drivers, and thereby stem the apparently rising tide of incidents involving their vehicles.

Since 1937, the System has formed the basis of all instruction given to police drivers, and in 1955 it became available to the general motoring public with the publication of the Roadcraft Manual. This first edition of Roadcraft was essentially simply an edited version of the teaching notes used by the police instructors. It has been revised, amended and reprinted on a regular basis since 1955, but the core remains unchanged. That core subject matter is the System of Car Control.

The System was formulated in recognition of the fact that a driver maximizes his chances of successfully dealing with a given hazard if, at the time he begins dealing with it, his vehicle is:

❑ in the correct position on the road,

❑ travelling at the correct speed, and

❑ has the correct gear engaged.

If any one or more of these states is not correctly established then the driver has only a reduced chance of safely dealing with the problem posed.

Examples of situations where the driver has failed to correctly establish each of these three criteria and thus failed to deal with the hazard safely would be as follows:

❑ The driver passes very close to a line of stationary vehicles. Because of this poor position he is unable to see a child standing between two of the vehicles and has a reduced reaction time should the child step out. The child does step out and a collision occurs.

❑ The driver enters a bend at too high a speed. Because of the high speed he is unable to negotiate the bend and leaves the road.

❏ The driver commences an overtake but is in a high, unresponsive gear. Consequently, with poor acceleration the manoeuvre takes longer than necessary and danger is caused by the approach of an oncoming vehicle.

It can be seen from the above examples that the three factors of position, speed, and gear, are very closely related to each other. For instance, it may have been safe for the driver in the first example to pass very close to the stationary vehicles providing he did so at a much reduced speed.

Likewise, it may have been safe for the driver in the second example to enter the bend at a high speed providing he did so from a different position on the road, and for the driver in the third example to perform the overtake in the high gear providing his initial speed was higher.

This leads to a further crucial point concerning the design of The System. It is not simply the actual elements of The System (Position, Speed, and Gear) which are of importance. Rather, of equal significance is the order in which these three elements are established. It has been seen elsewhere that the gear selected is dependent upon the speed set, and it is now clear that the correct speed with which to deal with a particular hazard cannot be assessed until the position from which it will be approached has been decided.

Thus, by driving to the System of Car Control the driver ensures that he first sets the correct position or course on which to approach a hazard; that on the basis of this he then sets the correct speed; and finally, that on the basis of the speed of his vehicle he engages the correct gear.

What is a hazard?

A hazard is any situation which the driver identifies as containing an element of actual or potential danger. The degree of danger is irrelevant: whenever any amount is identified as existing the driver needs to implement the problem solving procedure and establish the correct position, speed, and gear with which to deal with it.

The earlier the driver is able to carry out these tasks of hazard identification and resolution the smoother and more gentle will be the adjustments he makes to his position or speed, and the more time he will have for his gear change.

The mark of the advanced driver is his ability to identify and then prepare his vehicle for the next hazard at such an early stage that changes to any of its states are smooth, undramatic, and unhurried. The advanced driver would 'drift' his vehicle over to the left and simply decelerate for the next right hand bend, whereas the non-advanced driver would leave both these movements so late that a formal turn to the left was required and it was found to be necessary to brake.

A driver may identify hazards within hazards. A primary hazard may contain one or more secondary hazards. As the driver turns off a roundabout, for example, and enters a busy high street awash with vehicles and shoppers, that stretch of road represents to him a primary hazard. He must position his vehicle correctly, slow down to the appropriate speed and then engage the correct gear with which to deal with it.

Within that stretch of road individual secondary hazardous elements may emerge (a pedestrian stepping into the road, for instance, or one of the parked cars moving away) which require an individual setting of position, speed, and gear. Once that isolated hazard has been resolved, then in the absence of any further secondary hazards the driver would consider returning to the original position, speed, and gear established for the primary hazard.

Hazardous elements are classified under three headings:

❏ Physical features, such as a junction, roundabout, bend, or hill crest;

❏ Those created by the position or movement of other road users such as cyclists, pedestrians, animals, or other drivers;

❏ Those created by variations in road surface or weather conditions such as a patch of wet leaves, surface water, a bank of fog, or bright sunlight.

It is clearly possible for a single overall hazard to be a combination either of individual elements from two or more separate categories, or of two or more elements from the same category. Turning right into a side road with the presence of oncoming traffic, and a loose road surface at the apex of the turn, is an example of the first such type of situation (an element from each of the three categories), and an oncoming vehicle moving out to pass a cyclist would be an example of the second (two elements from the second category).

Definition of 'The System'

The System is defined as follows:

A system or drill, each feature of which is considered, in sequence, by the driver at the approach to any hazard.

This definition will now be examined:

The words 'drill' and 'in sequence' are important and revealing. They suggest firstly that a certain amount of discipline is required when using The System (which it is), and secondly that use of it will be basically repetitive. Each time the driver implements The System in order to deal with a hazard, he does so in basically the same way as he did the time before – he begins at the beginning and ends at the end.

The great benefit of having this preordained, logical, and repetitive sequence of actions to perform is that once it has been shown to work successfully the driver knows that he can trust it, and that all that is required of him is to make sure he uses the problem solving tool correctly. He may rest assured that all the factors which need considering on the approach to a hazard will be considered if he simply works through the various features of The System in sequence.

If a driver were to approach each hazard differently to the one before, and more or less ad lib his way through it, then the probability is high that some crucial consideration would be omitted. Human beings are essentially creatures of habit. When a routine has been shown to work then for very good reasons they tend to stick with it.

Note should be taken of the word 'considered' in the above definition. Although the object of the System is to ensure that the driver gives some thought to all aspects of his vehicle's state on the approach to the next hazard, it will not always be necessary for him to adjust every aspect of it.

For instance, he may already be in a suitable position from which to pass the next stationary obstruction; his speed may already be correct for the next bend; or he may already be in the correct gear to make the next turn. When this is the case the driver simply ignores the feature of The System dealing with that aspect and moves on to the next. By requiring, however, that he does at least 'consider' every aspect there is no danger of any detail being omitted and, for instance, him entering the next bend in the wrong gear simply because he neglected to give any thought to his gear.

Also of great importance are the words 'at the approach to any hazard'. It is vital that the vehicle is prepared for the next hazard before the driver actually commences dealing with it.

To adjust any of position, speed, or gear while actually negotiating the hazard will mean that the vehicle is to a greater or lesser extent destabilized. It is therefore under reduced control at precisely the time that stability and control should be maximized, i.e. in the hazard itself.

The disadvantages of, for instance, altering the direction of the vehicle while travelling over a poor road surface; braking while negotiating a bend; or changing gear while passing a group of lively children playing on the left, have been discussed elsewhere. The great advantage which systematic drivers have over those not so disciplined, is that all adjustments to their vehicles are made prior to entering the hazard which they have identified, and thus at the time of maximum safety.

Abiding by this aspect of the definition of the System, and completing all changes to the state of his vehicle on the approach to the hazard also brings another advantage. It ensures that the driver has the time to complete these changes of state properly and safely. For instance, if a junction is entered at too high a speed and a problem arises, the driver may not have time to check his mirrors before applying the brakes, thereby risking a rear end shunt. Had he slowed his vehicle down on the approach to the junction in plenty of time, he would have had the opportunity to do the manoeuvre properly and consult his mirrors before reducing speed.

*The correct position, speed and gear should be established **before** reaching the hazard . . .*

. . . this means that the hazard is actually negotiated with both hands on the steering wheel and the vehicle is under full control.

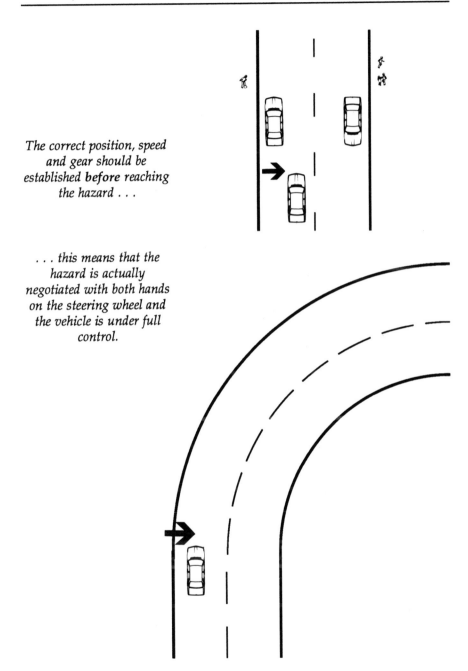

For a driver to be able to drive in this fashion, i.e. planning his drive in advance rather than responding to situations only once he is actually upon them, requires of him good observation and anticipation. These matters are covered in Chapter 6.

The Features of The System

The six features of the System are as follows:

1. Course

Having identified a hazard ahead the driver decides upon the correct line of approach. If achieving the correct line requires him to alter his present direction or position then all round observation is taken and consideration given to the need for a deviation signal to warn other road users of this fact.

2. Mirrors, Signals, Speed

With the vehicle on the correct line of approach, the correct speed is now established. If this requires a change in speed then all round observation is taken and consideration given to the need for a signal to warn other road users of this fact.

3. Gear

The correct gear for the chosen road speed is now selected.

4. Mirrors and Signals

If negotiation of the hazard requires a further manoeuvre (e.g. the actual turn of the vehicle into the new road when making a left or right turn) then all round observation is again taken and consideration given to the need for signals to warn of this intention.

5. Horn

If it is considered necessary to warn another road user of his presence, at this point the driver should sound his horn or flash his headlamps.

6. Acceleration

If the situation remains safe then the hazard is negotiated under the appropriate amount of acceleration.

If at any time during the implementation of the System on the approach to a hazard the circumstances should change, e.g. a vehicle appears in the mouth of the side road on the right into which the driver was preparing to turn, then the driver should begin to deal with what is now essentially a new hazard by reverting to Feature 1 of the System and beginning again. Often in this type of situation few of the features when considered for a second time would be required, because those established the first time would still be good.

They **must**, however, all be considered. In the example given above, if, for instance, the vehicle appeared during the driver's implementation of Feature 4, reverting to Features 1, 2 and 3 would probably only require the application of an indicator before moving on to the remaining features and completing the turn. In this type of case, in normal circumstances, the position, speed, and gear previously set prior to the arrival of the other vehicle would still be the ones required. If one or more are not the ones required then they should be adjusted in accordance with the features of the System.

It should be clear that the System of Car Control is a simple routine to both understand and use. It is, in essence, simply the 'mirrors-signals-manoeuvre' sequence discussed previously, used three times over. That is:

❏ All round observation is taken and consideration given to the need for signals before altering course (Feature 1);

❏ All round observation is taken and consideration given to the need for signals before altering speed (Feature 2);

❏ All round observation is taken and consideration given to the need for signals before carrying out the turn itself (Features 4, 5 and 6).

A number of ancillary points regarding the use of the System now need to be made.

❏ On each occasion that a signal is considered (i.e. Features 1, 2 and 4) signals warning both of the intention to carry out the immediate manoeuvre and a subsequent one are considered.

For instance, in the situation where a left turn is being made into a side road and the only other road users in the vicinity are a group of children standing in the side road, then in this instance an indicator would be applied at Feature 2 – not to warn them of any intention on the driver's part to reduce speed (i.e. not to warn them of the very next manoeuvre he will be carrying out) but rather to warn them of the actual turn into the road, i.e. the Feature 6 manoeuvre.

Similarly, in the situation where a right turn is to be made into a side road and the only other road user in the vicinity is a driver wishing to emerge from that side road and turn right, then a right-hand indicator would be applied at Feature 1, not to warn the other driver of the immediate move out to the right (i.e. not to warn him of the very next manoeuvre to be carried out) because he probably does not require warning or informing of that, but rather to warn him of the future manoeuvre of slowing down (Feature 2) and actually turning (Feature 6). The most useful to him of these two would probably be the warning of the reduction of speed at Feature 2, because on the basis of this he may then decide there is sufficient time for him to emerge safely before the arrival of the turning vehicle. (See Chapter 3 for the implication within an indicator of a reduction in speed.)

❑ If a signal is given at an early feature in the application of the System, e.g. an indicator at Feature 1, then the subsequent considerations of signals at later features (i.e. 2 and 4) still need to be made in order to decide whether it is necessary to confirm the one already given.

For instance, when turning right opposite a parked vehicle, an indicator activated at Feature 1 or 2 may need to be later confirmed by an arm signal at Feature 4 in order to clarify that the intention is to actually turn rather than simply move out to pass the obstruction.

❑ As seen in Chapter 3, the only signal which would warn directly of an intention to reduce speed at Feature 2 is a slowing down arm signal. An indicator only contains an implication of a reduction in speed, and brake lights only appear once the vehicle has begun slowing.

❏ Although systematic driving is desirable and provides the greatest safety margins in the negotiation of hazards, if at any time the driver finds that it is necessary in the interests of safety to carry out an operation which is not, strictly speaking, systematic, then The System must be ignored and that operation performed.

For instance, it will be seen that correct implementation of the System will provide for only one period of braking per hazard. If, however, the driver makes a misjudgement, and after Feature 3 he is still travelling too fast to make, for instance, the planned left turn, then the brakes must be re-applied. The fact that secondary braking should not be required takes second place to the safety of the manoeuvre. The driver in this situation should take effective observation, re-apply the brakes, carry out the manoeuvre safely, and then allocate time in future to practise making his left turns correctly.

Full, proper and habitual implementation of the System of Car Control only comes with practice. To those drivers unfamiliar with it, it will appear very daunting and intimidating. Surprise is often expressed at the fact that it is even possible to carry out the logical progression of these six separate and distinct steps on the approach to **every** hazard. The cry is often heard, *"I haven't got time to do all that"*.

The truth is that most drivers do not have sufficient time because they do not give themselves sufficient time. Through a combination of poor observation and poor forward planning, many drivers find themselves responding to situations only when they are very close to, or even in the middle of, that situation. To drive systematically the driver needs to begin the problem solving procedure well before arriving at the hazard he has identified. In order to do that he needs to be observing and assessing the hazard at an early stage. Thus, systematic driving demands of the driver good observation and forward planning. Likewise, good observation and forward planning enable the driver to drive systematically and safely.

Once systematic driving has been mastered, the driver ceases to think in terms of the individual features of the system, of their particular number or elements. Rather he responds automatically to the situation, safely establishing the correct position, speed, and gear with which to deal with it. The stage is eventually reached where he finds it virtually impossible to drive in any way other than this; where he is about as likely to make a gear change before he has set his speed as he is to begin any other form of behaviour which is totally alien to him.

The System is simply the logical outcome of applying the principles discussed elsewhere in this book. If all the other principles are accepted, then The System must also be accepted. The System of Car Control is simply *Mirrors-Signals-Manoeuvre*.

Appendix

Below are transcribed two commentary drives. They relate to the same drive over the same stretch of road.

It may be seen that commentary (a), although seeming to give a clear, logical, and sequential description of the driver's actions, is in fact based predominantly in the past tense. The driver informs the listener of many actions which he has taken, and of many factors along the route which have already changed. Commentary (b), by comparison, is centred almost entirely in the present and future tenses. It demonstrates clearly this driver's more forward observation and planning, and allows the listener to more accurately understand the reasoning behind his various actions.

The driver providing commentary (a) also demonstrates a much more limited field of vision, particularly ahead of his vehicle. He fails to observe many details which would assist him in anticipating the likely outcome of situations. He shows a tendency to deal with one hazard, and only then look ahead for the next. The driver providing commentary (b), on the other hand, reveals an understanding of the fact that there is no such thing as irrelevant information, and that the earlier he can gather this information the more accurate may be his assessment of it, and thus the more help may it provide.

Commentary (a)

"I'm now moving away from the side of the road. There wasn't anybody around who would have benefited from an indicator so it was not necessary to give one.

This is a fairly narrow road with private house driveways to the right and left. It is now going gently downhill and the centre lines which were present when I moved off have just changed to hazard lines.

I'm in third gear at the moment and I'll stay in that gear because there is a cyclist on the right with one vehicle behind. The cyclist is wobbling a little bit so I'll keep my speed down. Because it's very narrow I've had to slow down in fact, so I'll take second gear. I'm now moving gently past. The car behind the cyclist had tucked in and stayed there, and there was no need for any other signals.

There is a warning sign on the left for a roundabout. It is my intention to follow the road ahead which is the first exit. I can see in fact that it is a mini-roundabout, and this is confirmed by the sign I am passing. Mirror check, one vehicle behind. Although I can see along the road I will be joining, I've not had any view yet along the road to the right so I've had to slow right down. It was clear so I took second gear and I'm driving away. Even though there was one following vehicle no indicator was necessary to leave the roundabout.

The road is continuing to go gently downhill, and the driveways are still close to the left and right. It's fairly quiet at the moment. I'm just passing a junction on the left but it seems to be clear and presents no dangers.

There is a warning triangle on the left for road narrows from both sides. Mirror check. No following traffic. The vehicle which was behind me must have turned off at the roundabout. I've come off the gas pedal now because the hill is sufficient to take me down at a safe speed. I can see where the road narrows, and in fact it is a hump bridge. Mirror check. I've had to take second gear because with the restricted view I've had to lose a lot of speed. Gently over the hill. Once the view had opened up there was no need for a horn warning.

The road ahead is now bending to the left. Mirror check, no following traffic. The hill is pulling me around the bend. All the parked vehicles I passed were empty and again I didn't need a horn note.

I'm staying well into the left and now rounding a right-hand bend. Mirror check. All clear.

Driving round the bend now and re-applying a little gas because the gentle hill has flattened out. Passing parked vehicles.

There is a road junction on the left with one vehicle approaching. It slowed down but I covered the brake just in case. There was no following traffic.

I'm now almost at a T-junction. I'm turning left. I've indicated for the benefit of following traffic, and I'm ready to stop because I can't see to the right. In fact it is clear both ways so it was OK to move away in second gear.

This is a busier road than the previous one. There is traffic ahead and a set of traffic lights on green. Mirror check. One following vehicle. I'm keeping third gear through the lights. They turned out to be a Pelican crossing.

I am coming to another set of traffic lights on red. I intend to turn left at the junction. Mirror check. Following traffic a good way behind. I'm stopping at the line. The opposing traffic is still going through.

Mirror check. I'll put a left indicator on now because the following traffic has caught up and stopped behind. My lights are changing so I've put it into first gear and I'm moving away.

My new road is of similar description to the last. There are parked vehicles on either side. I'm accelerating away..."

Commentary (b)

"I am now ready to move away from the side of the road. I'm making a physical check of blind spots over both left and right shoulders. There is nobody anywhere who would benefit from an indicator, so I'm removing the handbrake and moving away.

This is a fairly narrow road and is beginning to descend a gentle hill. Looking ahead I can see a warning sign, but I can't at the moment read what it says. I'll look at it again when I'm nearer. Up into third gear. Centre lines will be changing shortly to hazard lines. That would fit in with the warning sign. Private house driveways on either side. Most of them are obscured by walls and hedges so I'm keeping my speed down because I would get little or no warning of anything emerging.

Looking ahead I can see a young cyclist on the right. She's wobbling a little bit. Mirror check. No following traffic. Off the gas pedal. There is now an oncoming vehicle nearing the cyclist. There isn't room for the three of us to pass safely abreast so another mirror check and I'm going to brake. The oncoming vehicle has tucked in behind the cyclist and I'm happy that he will be staying there. I'll take second gear. Mirror check. All clear behind, and I'm accelerating gently past the two of them.

I can now read the warning triangle which is for a roundabout. It's backed up by a mini-roundabout sign. Mirror check. One following vehicle a good distance behind. It is my intention to follow the road ahead at the roundabout, which is the first exit. Mirror check. Following vehicle closing. I'm keeping well to the left to maximize my view into the road on the right, and I'm braking gently. No view to the right at the moment so more brakes. Clear ahead. Now I've got the view, it's all clear. I'll take second gear. Mirror check. Still one following vehicle. Accelerating gently into the roundabout. No need for an indicator to leave.

The road is continuing downhill, driveways still very close left and right. Up into third gear. Looking ahead I can see a warning sign, obscured by a telegraph pole at present. There is a side road on the left, and the view into it is beginning to open up. Mirror check. The following vehicle is turning off to the right at the roundabout.

Looking ahead at the street lamps the road appears to bend to the left. I can now read the warning sign and it is for road narrows from both sides. The junction on the left is empty. Mirror check. No following traffic. Coming off the gas and letting the hill take me down. I can see where the road narrows. It is a hump bridge followed immediately by a bend to the left. Mirror check. Braking gently because I don't have a view over the bridge yet. Speed is right now. I'll take second gear. I'm considering a horn note but the view is now opening up and one is not necessary.

It's all clear on the far side. I can see the bend to the left and it's quite sharp. Two parked vehicles on the right. Both appear empty, no sign of any feet underneath. Mirror check. No following traffic. Tucking well into the left and braking slightly. I'm going to stay in second gear and let the hill pull me round. No need for a horn warning.

I'm going to stay well into the left because I can see that the road will soon be bending round to the right. There's a warning triangle for a school playground so I'm looking out for children and dogs etcetera. Mirror check. All clear.

The gentle downhill which I've had since setting off is beginning to flatten out, so I'll apply gentle gas to take me around the bend. As it straightens out I'll now increase the gas.

Looking ahead I can see a T-junction at approximately 300 yards. Parked vehicles left and right, all appear empty. Prior to the T-junction is a road on the left, with one vehicle approaching the Give Way lines. Mirror check. Clear behind. I'm off the gas and covering the brake pedal. The brake lights have illuminated on that vehicle and I can see the driver looking in my direction. I'm now happy he is stopping. Mirror check. All clear. Back on the gas and drive past.

Nearing the T-junction. It is my intention to turn left. Mirror check. The vehicle has emerged from the road on the left and I will indicate for his benefit. No view to the right as yet, but I can see that it is clear to the left. The road I will be joining has hazard lines along its centre.

Mirror check. Gentle braking. The view to the right has now opened up. It's all clear. Another check left and right. I'll take second gear. Near-side door mirror check. All clear, moving away.

Accelerating away and up into third gear. I've got one vehicle approximately fifty yards ahead and I can see two sets of traffic lights, both presently on green. There is a pedestrian precinct on the right, fairly busy at the moment. Several oncoming vehicles.

I'm now up to thirty miles per hour, but I'm going to keep it in third gear because the first set of traffic lights is a Pelican crossing, and I can see two elderly people standing near the crossing on the right. Mirror check. One following vehicle. Off the gas pedal and covering the brake. The pedestrian Wait sign on the right is illuminated so the lights are due to change. I am now committed but I am keeping an eye on the pedestrians.

The second set of traffic lights is showing red. This is a junction and it is my intention to turn left. My position is correct. Mirror check. The pedestrian lights have now changed and following traffic is stopping. I am applying a left-hand indicator because I can see that the opposing lights are still on green and following traffic will be moving up behind me shortly. Off the gas pedal, gentle braking and I will stop in my approach gear.

I've got a good view of the road I will be turning into. It's of similar size to this one with a line of parked vehicles on either side. No sign of any movement around them. Mirror check. Following traffic is pulling up safely. The opposing lights are now changing, so I'll take first gear. None of the oncoming traffic is indicating right. Off with the handbrake. Mirror check including the left-hand door mirror in case of a cyclist or motor-cyclist moving up there. Keeping it in first gear around the turn, but now I've straightened up I'll select second.

Mirror check. No vehicles have followed me around so it is safe to accelerate away..."

The Royal Society for the Prevention of Accidents

△ RoSPA
**DRIVER
SERVICES**

Are you responsible for transport management?

If so, RoSPA Driver Services can help reduce costs by improving the efficiency of your fleet — and the safety of your drivers. Your insurance claims record should get better — leading to lower premiums

WE OFFER

- **Defensive Driver Training** • **Driver Assessments**
- **The Advanced Driving Test** • **National Safe Driving Awards Scheme**
- **Personal Safety Courses** • **Skid Control Courses**

DRIVER TRAINING IS A HIGH RETURN INVESTMENT

For details of how we can help please contact: Roger Clark, on 021-200 2461 or 05297-262

△ RoSPA
**DRIVER
SERVICES**

Why cannot we
use 4th gear, or
3rd Gear whatever.

* because (pupil) cannot see ahead
clearly, could be a car broke broke
down, cyclist - the middle of the
way, or another could be a
car can coming to one side of the
road,

50 BEST CYCLE RIDES IN CHESHIRE
- edited by Graham Beech

- all of these walking and cycling books are currently £6.95 each.

For long-distance walks enthusiasts, we have several books including:

THE GREATER MANCHESTER BOUNDARY WALK
- Graham Phythian

THE THIRLMERE WAY
- Tim Cappelli

THE MARCHES WAY
- Les Lumsdon

- all £6.95 each

We also publish:

A guide to the 'Pubs of Old Lancashire'

A fabulous series of 'Pub Walks' books all featuring access by public transport

A new series of investigations into the Supernatural, Myth and Magic

Superb illustrated books on Manchester's football teams

- plus many more entertaining and educational books being regularly added to our list.

All of our books are available from your local bookshop. In case of difficulty, or to obtain our complete catalogue, please contact:

Sigma Leisure,

1 South Oak Lane,

Wilmslow, Cheshire SK9 6AR

Phone: 0625 - 531035 Fax: 0625 - 536800

ACCESS and VISA orders welcome - call our friendly sales staff or use our 24 hour Answerphone service! Most orders are despatched on the day we receive your order - you could be enjoying our books in just a couple of days.

AUTHORS: if you have an interesting idea for a book, contact us for a rapid and expert decision. Note that we are not a 'Vanity Press' - all of our books earn royalties for their writers.